NESTORIUS

NESTORIUS

AND HIS PLACE IN THE
HISTORY OF CHRISTIAN DOCTRINE

by

FRIEDRICH LOOFS, D.D., Phil.D.

Professor of Church History in the University
of Halle-Wittenberg, Germany

Cambridge:

at the University Press

1914

CAMBRIDGE
UNIVERSITY PRESS

University Printing House, Cambridge CB2 8BS, United Kingdom

Cambridge University Press is part of the University of Cambridge.

It furthers the University's mission by disseminating knowledge in the pursuit of
education, learning and research at the highest international levels of excellence.

www.cambridge.org
Information on this title: www.cambridge.org/9781107450769

First published 1914
First paperback edition 2014

A catalogue record for this publication is available from the British Library

ISBN 9781107450769 Paperback

Cambridge University Press has no responsibility for the persistence or accuracy of
URLs for external or third-party internet websites referred to in this publication,
and does not guarantee that any content on such websites is, or will remain, accurate
or appropriate.

PREFACE

IN this small book I publish four lectures which I was invited to give in a course of "advanced lectures in theology" at the University of London, March, 1913. The lectures were for the most part originally written in German. I translated them with the kind assistance of Miss Ida Southhall, M.A., of Birmingham, then a guest at my house. But it is not she alone to whom I am indebted. I have also to thank my dear host during my stay in London, Professor H. J. White, who read two of my lectures before I gave them, and the corrector of the Cambridge University Press and two of our American students, Mr H. Harper, B.A., of Avalan (U.S.A.), and Mr Charles Baillie, B.D., of Picton (Canada), whose kind suggestions I often utilized in reading the proofs. However, I beg my readers to put it to my account, that in spite of all these friendly helpers, the German author very often reveals himself.

In quoting Nestorius' "Book of Heraclides" I have given the pages both of the Syriac text and of Nau's French translation—not in order to raise in my reader's mind the idea that I made use of the Syriac text.

Having forgotten nearly all I once knew of Syriac,
I examined the Syriac text with the help of various
friends only in a very few places, and I realize how
much the ordinary use of the French translation alone
is to be regarded as a defect in my lectures. I have
quoted the numbers of the pages of the original Syriac
text, as given by Nau, only in order that in this way
the places where the quotations are to be found may be
more accurately indicated than by merely quoting the
pages of Nau's translation.

Since this book went to press I have made the
acquaintance of a lecture by Dr Junglas, a Roman-
Catholic scholar, entitled *Die Irrlehre des Nestorius*
(Trier, 1912, 29 pages), and of the interesting chapters
on "the tragedy of Nestorius" and "the council of
Chalcedon" in. L. Duchesne's *Histoire ancienne de
l'Église* (tom. III, Paris, 1911, pp. 313–388 and 389–
454). The latter makes little use of the newly
discovered *Liber Heraclidis* and does not give much
detail about the teaching of Nestorius. Nevertheless
I regret very much that I did not know earlier this
treatment of the matter, surely more learned and more
impartial than any other of Roman-Catholic origin.
Dr Junglas in giving a short delineation of Nestorius'
"heresy" has utilized the "Book of Heraclides" and,
in my opinion, made some valuable remarks about the
terminology of Nestorius which are not to be found
elsewhere. However, in his one short lecture he was

not able to go into details, and there are many things which he has failed to observe. There is a third Roman-Catholic research into the doctrine of Nestorius (Jugie, article " Éphèse, concile de" in the *Dictionnaire de la théologie catholique*, Fasc. 37, Paris, 1911, pp. 137–163), which, as I understand, endeavours more eagerly than Dr Junglas to show that Nestorius was justly condemned; but I have not had the opportunity to read this article.

As regards my own treatment of the matter, I do not pretend to have exhausted the subject nor to have found the definite and final answers to the various questions aroused about Nestorius' life and doctrine by his *Liber Heraclidis*. I trust that I have indicated more clearly than Professor Bethune-Baker has already done the way by which we may arrive at a real understanding of Nestorius' peculiar ideas. Others, I hope, may be stimulated by the present lectures to a further study of Nestorius' christology. The subject is deserving of interest. For there is no other christology in the ancient church so "modern" as his and perhaps that of his teachers whose dogmatical works are lost.

F. L.

HALLE ON THE SAALE, GERMANY,
January 20th, 1914.

I

THE subject of my lectures—"Nestorius and his position in the history of Christian Doctrine"—seems at the first glance to have little interest for us modern men. Almost 1500 years have passed since Nestorius played his rôle in history. And this rôle was in the orthodox church a very transitory one.

For the Persian-Nestorian or Syrian-Nestorian church (as the language of this church was Syriac) Nestorius, it is true, became a celebrated saint; and still to-day small remains of this once far-reaching church are to be found in the vicinity of the Urmia Lake in the north-west of Persia and south of it in the mountains of Turkish Kurdistan. But in the orthodox church Nestorius was even in his own time an ephemeral appearance. In the year 428 A.D. he became bishop of Constantinople and as early as 431 he was deposed. Four years later he was banished to Oasis in Egypt, and up to a few years ago the common opinion was that he died soon after in his exile.

For the orthodox church he remained merely one of the most condemned heretics. He was reproached not

only for having forbidden the title θεοτόκος, mother of
God, as applied to Mary the virgin, but it was told of
him that he, separating the divine and the human
nature of Christ, saw in our Saviour nothing but an
inspired man[1]. What was right in his statements, viz.
his opposition to all monophysitic thinking, was held to
be maintained by the famous letter of Leo the Great to
Flavian of Constantinople of the year 449, acknowledged by the council of Chalcedon, and by the creed of
that council itself. The rest of what he taught was
regarded as erroneous and not worth the notice of
posterity.

That this is not a tenable theory I hope to prove in
my lectures.

To-day it is my aim merely to show that just at the
present time different circumstances have led to the
awakening of a fresh interest in Nestorius.

The church of the ancient Roman Empire did not
punish its heretics merely by deposition, condemnation,
banishment and various deprivations of rights, but,
with the purpose of shielding its believers against
poisonous influence, it destroyed all heretical writings.
No work of Arius, Marcellus, Aetius and Eunomius *e.g.*,
not to speak of the earlier heretics, has been preserved
in more than fragments consisting of quotations by their
opponents. A like fate was purposed for the writings

---

[1] Comp. Socrates, h. e. 7, 32, 6 ed. Gaisford II, 806; Evagrius,
h. e. 1, 7 ed. Bidez and Parmentier, p. 14, 6.

of Nestorius: an edict of the Emperor Theodosius II, dating from the 30th of July 435 ordered them to be burnt[1]. Even the Persian church, about the same time won over to Nestorianism, had to suffer under this edict: only a few works of Nestorius came into its possession for translation into Syriac.

This we learn through Ebed-Jesu, metropolitan of Nisibis (†1318), the most famous theologian of the Nestorians in the middle ages and who has given us the most complete account of the writings of Nestorius. He introduces in his catalogue of Syrian authors[2] the notice about Nestorius with the following words: *Nestorius the patriarch wrote many excellent books which the blasphemers* (viz. the Antinestorians) *have destroyed.* As those which evaded destruction he mentions, besides the liturgy of Nestorius, *i.e.* one of the liturgies used by the Nestorians, which without doubt is wrongly ascribed to Nestorius, five works of the patriarch. The first of these is the book called *Tragedy*, the second the *Book of Heraclides*, the third the *Letter addressed to Cosmas*, the fourth a *Book of letters* and the fifth a *Book of homilies and sermons*.

For us the edict of Theodosius against the writings of Nestorius has had a still more important result. Until 1897 nothing was known about the second book

---

[1] Cod. Theodos. 16, 5, 66; Mansi, v, 413 f.

[2] J. S. Assemani, *Bibliotheca orientalis*, III, 1, p. 35 f.

mentioned by Ebed-Jesu, *i.e.* about the *Book of Hera-clides*. Also the *Letter addressed to Cosmas* mentioned third by Ebed-Jesu had to be counted and is still to be counted as lost[1]. Of the three other works ascribed by Ebed-Jesu to Nestorius we had and still have only fragments—occasional quotations in the works of his enemies and his friends.

Among the hostile writings in which we find such fragments are to be named especially the works of his chief opponent Cyril of Alexandria; then the proceedings of the council of Ephesus; then some works of Marius Mercator, a Latin writer who in the time of Nestorius lived in Constantinople and translated a series of quotations from Nestorius given by Cyril, three letters of Nestorius and also, but with considerable omissions, nine of his sermons; finally the church history of Evagrius (living about 590). The latter gives us[2] an account of two works of Nestorius dating from the time of his exile, one of which must be the *Tragedy*, while the other could not be identified up to the last ten years, and he inserts in his narration extracts from two interesting letters of the banished heretic. Among the friends who preserved for us fragments of Nestorius the Nestorians of later date played a very unimportant part. Important is a Latin work which has connection with the earliest friends of Nestorius, the so-called

---

[1] Comp. Hauck's *Real-Encyklopädie*, xxiv, 242, 56 ff.

[2] h. e. 1, 7 ed. Bidez and Parmentier, pp. 12 ff.

Synodicon, known since 1682[1] or, in complete form, since 1873[2], and which is a later adaptation of a work of Bishop Irenaeus of Tyrus, a partisan of Nestorius, which was entitled "Tragedy" like the lost "Tragedy" of Nestorius, upon which perhaps it was based.

The quotations of these enemies and friends represent, as I said, fragments of three books of Nestorius mentioned by Ebed-Jesu, viz. the *Book of letters,* the *Book of sermons* and the *Tragedy.* The first two of these three works of Nestorius need no further explanation. The third, the *Tragedy,* about which Evagrius and the *Synodicon* teach us, must have been a polemical work, in which Nestorius, as Evagrius says, defended himself against those *who blamed him for having introduced unlawful innovations and for having acted wrongly in demanding the council of Ephesus*[3]. The title which the book bears must have been chosen because Nestorius told here the tragedy of his life up to his banishment to Oasis in Egypt.

Fragments of other books of Nestorius not mentioned by Ebed-Jesu were not known to us ten years ago[4].

---

[1] Ch. Lupus, *Ad Ephesinum concilium variorum patrum epistolae,* 1682 = Mansi, v, 731–1022.

[2] *Bibliotheca Casinensis,* i, 49–84. [3] h. e. 1, 7, pp. 12, 24 f.

[4] We had, it is true, the Anathematisms of Nestorius against Cyril's Anathematisms, and a fragment of his λογίδια; but the Anathematisms probably were attached to a letter, and the λογίδια (short discourses) perhaps belonged to the *Book of homilies and sermons.*

All the fragments previously known and in addition to them more than 100 new fragments preserved especially by the Syrian-monophysitic literature I collected and edited in 1905 in a volume entitled *Nestoriana*[1]. It is with pleasure that here in England I mention the collaboration of the learned English scholar Stanley A. Cook, an expert in Syrian language and literature, without whose help I never could have used the Syriac texts in the British Museum. I will not speak long of the book which this help and that of a German scholar then at Halle, Dr G. Kampffmeyer, enabled me to compose. Three remarks only shall be made. Firstly: The Syriac fragments gave us knowledge of a book of Nestorius not mentioned by Ebed-Jesu, which was written in the form of a dialogue and which was certainly a comprehensive work, although the number of the fragments handed down to us is very small. The title of this work is *The Theopaschites*, that is, the man who thinks God had suffered, a title certainly chosen because Nestorius in this dialogue opposed the Cyrillian party, which he accused of holding a doctrine which imagined the God in Christ suffering.

Secondly: The introductory headings in the Syriac fragments of the sermons of Nestorius in combination with a reconstruction of the order of the leaves in the

[1] *Nestoriana.* Die Fragmente des Nestorius, gesammelt, untersucht und herausgegeben von F. Loofs. Mit Beiträgen von Stanley A. Cook und G. Kampffmeyer, Halle, 1905.

manuscripts used by Marius Mercator and by the
council of Ephesus, offered the possibility of arranging
the fragments of the sermons of Nestorius in such
a manner that more than 30 sermons could be clearly
discerned and that not a few of them were recognisable
in their essential contents and their characteristics.

Thirdly: By the help of the quotations I succeeded
in finding—as did also at almost the same time a
Catholic scholar[1] independently of me—the original
Greek of one sermon of Nestorius in a sermon preserved
in a manuscript at Dresden and printed in 1839 as
a work of Chrysostomus. It is a sermon on the high
priesthood of Christ in many respects especially characteristic of the teaching of Nestorius.

Thus my *Nestoriana* gave for the first time an
opportunity to survey the remains of the works of
Nestorius then accessible. They were the first factor
in arousing fresh interest in Nestorius. They inspired,
as the author himself says, the writing of a monograph
on the christology of Nestorius by a Roman Catholic
chaplain, Dr Leonhard Fendt[2].

But the second factor now to be treated is still
more important and surely more interesting. Let me
give some introductory remarks before treating the
subject itself.

[1] S. Haidacher, *Rede des Nestorius über Hebr.* 3. 1, *überliefert
unter dem Nachlass des hl. Chrysostomus* (*Zeitschrift für katholische
Theologie*, xxix, 1905, pp. 192–195).

[2] *Die Christologie des Nestorius*, Kempten, 1910.

Some few heretics of the ancient church were fortunately enabled long after their death to triumph over the condemnation or even destruction which the orthodox church pronounced against their writings.

Of Apollinaris of Laodicea, the heretic whose doctrine was to Nestorius a special cause of offence, we have still not a few writings because the Apollinarists secretly introduced the works of their master into the church literature, inscribing them with the names of orthodox authors of good renown, *e.g.* Athanasius, Julius of Rome, Gregorius Thaumaturgos. Since these *fraudes Apollinaristarum*[1], of which as early as the 6th century some church writers had an idea or at least a suspicion[2], were carefully examined, a small collection of works of Apollinaris could be made. Prof. Lietz-mann of Jena gave such a collection in his *Apollinaris von Laodicea* in the year 1904.

Severus of Antioch, the most conspicuous of the Monophysites of the 6th century, continued to be admired in the Syrian monophysite church, although the orthodox church had anathematized him. Hence not an unimportant part of the works of Severus translated into Syriac has been preserved, especially among the Syriac manuscripts of the British Museum.

---

[1] Comp. Leontius, *adversus fraudes Apollinaristarum*; Migne, ser. graec. 86, 1947–1976.

[2] Comp. the preceding note and Nestorius' *ad Constantinopolitanos* (F. Nau, *Nestorius, Le Livre d'Héraclide*, p. 374).

And, besides others[1], your famous countryman E. W. Brooks has, to the great advantage of historical science, begun the publication of this material[2].

Pelagius, the well-known western contemporary of Nestorius, whose doctrine Augustine opposed, wrote beside other smaller dogmatical works a large commentary on the Epistles of Saint Paul, the original text of which was held to be lost. An orthodox adaptation only of this work, as was the opinion of ancient and modern scholars, existed in a commentary regarded since olden times as belonging to the works of Hieronymus and it has been printed among them. But nobody took much notice of these commentaries; for because they were regarded as having been revised they could teach nothing new about Pelagius, and one could only make use of those thoughts which otherwise were known to be his. Lately we have come by curious bypaths to valuable knowledge about the Pelagius-commentary which we hope will soon put us in possession of the original text of Pelagius. The well-known Celtic scholar, Heinrich Zimmer, formerly professor at the University of Berlin († 1910), was led, as we see in his book *Pelagius in Irland* (1901), to traces of the original Pelagius-commentary by quotations in Irish manuscripts. He

---

[1] *e.g.* R. Duval in *Patrologia orientalis*, IV, 1, 1906.

[2] *The sixth book of the select letters of Severus, Patriarch of Antiochia in the Syriac version* etc., 2 vols., London, 1902–1904; Hymns in *Patrologia orientalis*, VI, 1, 1910.

even believed he had recovered the original commentary itself; for a manuscript which he found in the monastery of S. Gallen (Switzerland) in his opinion nearly resembled the original text, in spite of some additions, and showed that the *Pseudo-Hieronymus, i.e.* the form printed among the works of Hieronymus, was more authentic than was previously supposed. This judgment on the manuscript of S. Gallen and the *Pseudo-Hieronymus* proved, it is true, to be too optimistic. But the investigation, begun by Professor Zimmer, has been furthered by German and English scholars by means of extensive study of manuscripts. Professor A. Souter of Aberdeen, who played a prominent rôle in this research and who really succeeded in finding at Karlsruhe a manuscript of the original Pelagius-commentary, is right in hoping that he will be able to give to theological science the original text of Pelagius within a few years[1].

In a still more curious manner Priscillian, the first heretic, who in consequence of his being accused was finally put to death (385), has been enabled to speak to us in his own words. None of his writings were preserved; we only had the accounts of his opponents. Then there was suddenly found, 27 years ago, in the University library at Würzburg (Bavaria) a manuscript of the 5th or 6th century containing 11 treatises of the old heretic perfectly intact—the genuineness of which

[1] Comp. Hauck's *Real-Encyklopädie*, xxiv, 311.

cannot in the least be doubted. It must remain a riddle for us how this manuscript could be preserved without attention having been drawn to it. Nevertheless it is a matter of fact that these 11 treatises of Priscillian now, more than 1500 years after his death, can again be read; they were printed in the edition of the discoverer, Dr Georg Schepps, in 1889.

A similar fortune was prepared for Nestorius. A Syriac translation of his *Book of Heraclides* mentioned above, which was made about 540 A.D., is preserved in a manuscript, dating from about 1100, in the library of the Nestorian Patriarch at Kotschanes in Persian Turkestan. The American missionaries in the neighbourhood of the Urmia Lake having heard about this manuscript, attempted to gain further information about it, and in 1889 a Syrian priest, by name Auscha'nâ, succeeded in making secretly a hurried copy of the manuscript for the library of the missionaries at Urmia. One copy of this Urmia copy came into the University library of Strassburg, another into the possession of Professor Bethune-Baker of Cambridge; a fourth copy has been made directly after the original at Kotschanes for the use of the Roman Catholic editor, the well-known Syriac scholar Paul Bedjan.

The rediscovery of this work of Nestorius was first made known when the existence of the Strassburg manuscript was heard of, in 1897[1]. The publication of

[1] Comp. my *Nestoriana*, p. 4.

the Syriac text was delayed longer than scholars seemed to have had a right to hope. The first detailed notice of the work, therefore, was given by Professor Bethune-Baker in his work, *Nestorius and his teaching,* edited 1908. This scholar had been enabled by means of an English translation of a friend to make use of the *Book of Heraclides* or " Bazaar of Heraclides " as he called it. Long quotations from the book of Nestorius made this publication of great value. As late as 1910 the edition of the Syriac text by Paul Bedjan appeared and at the same time a French translation by F. Nau[1]. It is especially this publication which is able at the present time to arouse interest in Nestorius.

First the preface of the Syriac translator attracts our attention. The translator remarks at the conclusion that the following book of Nestorius belongs to the controversial writings on the faith and must be read after the " *Theopaschites* " and the " *Tragedy* ", *which he wrote as apologetic answers to those who had blamed him for having demanded a council*[2]. This remark not only confirms what we already knew from Evagrius about the *Tragedy* of Nestorius, but it enables us also to identify the second book of the banished Nestorius known to Evagrius. Evagrius tells us that it was directed against a certain Egyptian—Cyril is often

[1] *Nestorius, Le Livre d'Héraclide de Damas,* ed. P. Bedjan, Paris, 1910; *Nestorius, Le Livre d'Héraclide de Damas, traduit en Français par* F. Nau, Paris, 1910.

[2] Bedjan, p. 4; Nau, p. 3.

called by Nestorius "the Egyptian"—and that it was
written διαλεκτικῶς[1], apparently meaning "in the form
of a dialogue". These words of Evagrius even before the
discovery of the *Book of Heraclides* could be held to point
to the *Theopaschites*, which has in the fragments that
are preserved the dialogue form. Nevertheless in my
Nestoriana I did not venture to make this identification
because the book known to Evagrius must have also
contained historical-polemical passages, while the fragments we have present no such material. Now according
to the preface of the translator of the *Book of Heraclides*
the *Theopaschites* really contained historical-polemical
material. One can therefore now without doubt identify
it with the second book notified by Evagrius.

More interesting than the preface is naturally the
book itself. Its title, "*Tegurtâ*" of *Heraclides of
Damascus*, according to Bedjan[2] and Nau[3] corresponding in Greek to Πραγματεία Ἡρακλείδου τοῦ
Δαμασκηνοῦ, hence "Treatise of Heraclides"—not
"Bazaar of Heraclides" as Professor Bethune-Baker
translated—is the most puzzling thing in the whole
work. The Syriac translator remarks in his preface that
Heraclides was a noble and educated man living in the
neighbourhood of Damascus, and that Nestorius puts
this name in the title of his book because he feared

---

[1] h. e. 1, 7, pp. 13, 21: γράφει δὲ καὶ ἕτερον λόγον πρός τινα δῆθεν
Αἰγύπτιον συγκείμενον κ.τ.λ. [2] p. viii, no. 2.

[3] p. xvii and *Revue de l'Orient chrétien*, XIV, 1909, pp. 208 f.

that his own name would prevent people from reading it[1]. The Syriac translator therefore had already found the title *Treatise of Heraclides* in his Greek original. He does not seem to have known anything about the meaning of this title. The vague remarks he makes about Heraclides tell nothing more than anyone might guess without his help. The book itself in its present incomplete condition—about one-sixth of the whole is missing—nowhere explains the title, Heraclides not being mentioned at all. And Nestorius has made no effort to conceal his authorship. The names of the persons which, in the dialogue of the first part of the book, head the single portions of the text, viz. *Nestorius* and *Sophronius*, must, it is true, be regarded as later additions—just as the headings of the chapters. But the manner in which the matter is dealt with, especially in the second half of the book, reveals so clearly that Nestorius is the writer, that a pseudonym, as *Heraclides* or anyone else, could have deceived only those who gave no attention to the contents. Perhaps—that is the opinion of Bethune-Baker[2]—the pseudonymous title is to be regarded as the device of an adherent of Nestorius, to save his master's apology from destruction.

However it may be—the book itself has nothing to do with Heraclides of Damascus. It falls, as the Syriac translator rightly remarks[3], into two parts, the first of

[1] Bedjan, p. 3; Nau, p. 3.
[2] *Nestorius and his teaching*, p. 33.   [3] Bedjan, p. 4; Nau, p. 4.

which has three, the second two sections. To the first section of the first part[1] the translator gives the heading: *Of all heresies opposed to the church and of all the differences with regard to the faith of the 318 (i.e.* the Fathers of Nicaea). In the second section[2] Nestorius, as the translator observes, *attacks Cyril and criticizes the judges* (who condemned him) *and the charges of Cyril.* The third section[3] contains according to the translator *his* (viz. Nestorius') *answer* (or apology) *and a comparison of their letters* (viz. of Cyril and Nestorius). The first section of the second part[4] is characterized by the translator as *a refutation and rectification of all charges for which he was excommunicated,* and the second section[5] as dealing with the time or the events *from his excommunication to the close of his life.*

Even the first of the five sections shows considerable omissions; the second is incomplete in the beginning and again at the end; also of the third section the beginning is missing. The fourth section, in which all extracts from the sermons of Nestorius criticized at Ephesus as heretical are brought under review, seems, apart from small omissions, incomplete only in the

---

[1] Bedjan, pp. 10–13 f.; Nau, pp. 1–88; comp. Hauck's *Real-Encyklopädie,* xxiv, 240, 44 ff.

[2] Bedjan, pp. 147–209; Nau, pp. 88–125.

[3] Bedjan, pp. 209–270; Nau, pp. 126–163.

[4] Bedjan, pp. 138–160 and 271–366 (or 459); Nau, pp. 163–235 (or 294); comp. Hauck's *Real-Encyklopädie,* xxiv, 240, 55 f.

[5] Bedjan, 366 (or 459)–521; Nau, 235 (or 294)–331.

beginning; the last section is the most completely preserved.

In spite of all omissions it is a book of extensive scope in which Nestorius speaks to us: the Syriac text has 521 pages, the French translation of Nau fills 331, and they are of a large size.

In reading the book one has to regret, it is true, again and again, that it has not been preserved intact and in its original language. It would be of inestimable importance for the history of Christian doctrine if we possessed the original Greek of these explanations, so important from a dogmatic point of view.

Nevertheless even as we have it now in the Syriac translation the *Treatise of Heraclides* of Nestorius remains one of the most interesting discoveries for students of ancient church history. In two respects it is able to awaken fresh interest in Nestorius: by what we hear about his life and by what we learn about his doctrine.

As concerning the first, the *Treatise of Heraclides* has undoubtedly many relations to that earlier work of Nestorius, entitled *Tragedy* and only known in a few fragments, in which he treated historically and polemically the tragedy of his life and especially the doings of the Cyrillian council of Ephesus. Also in the *Treatise of Heraclides* Nestorius writes as one who is conscious of being unjustly condemned and wrongly delivered over to the intrigues of the unscrupulous

Cyril. But he does not make pretentious claims for his person or hope for another turn of his fortune. He has no more interest in the world. For *e.g.* after having said that one might ask him why the bishops of the Antiochian party had given assent to his deposition he answers[1]: *Well you must ask him* (meaning Cyril), *apparently also those* (meaning the Antiochians). *If you want to learn anything else of me, then I will speak of what is now gradually coming to the knowledge of the whole world, not in order to find approbation or assistance among men—for earthly things have but little interest for me. I have died to the world and live for Him, to whom my life belongs;—but I will speak to those who took offence* etc. He writes in exile in the deserts of Egypt and has no prospect but of death. *As for me,* so he concludes the treatise[2], *I have borne the sufferings of my life and all that has befallen me in this world as the sufferings of a single day; and I have not changed all these years. And now I am already on the point to depart, and daily I pray to God to dismiss me—me whose eyes have seen his salvation. Farewell Desert, my friend, mine upbringer and my place of sojourning, and thou Exile, my mother, who after my death shalt keep my body until the resurrection comes in the time of God's pleasure! Amen.*

We knew previously that Nestorius had to endure

---

[1] Bedjan, p. 451; Nau, p. 289.
[2] Bedjan, p. 520 f.; Nau, p. 331.

many sufferings during his exile. Evagrius, as I said
above, hands down to us fragments of two letters of
Nestorius to the governor of Thebais[1]. From these
we learn that Nestorius was captured in Oasis by
invading bands of barbarians and then, being released,
surrendered himself, by a letter written in Panopolis, into
the hands of the governor, in order not to come under
the suspicion of having fled. But then, so the second
letter teaches us, he was sent by order of the governor
first to Elephantine and, before reaching it, back to
Panopolis, then into the surrounding district and from
there to a fourth place of exile. The hardships of these
continual removals and severe bodily pains caused by an
injured hand and side had brought him to the brink of
death. We cannot help being moved when we see him
in his first letter from Panopolis, written directly after
his release from capture, asking the governor that he
should see to a lawful continuation of his exile, *lest in
all future generations should be told the tragic history
that it was better to be captured by barbarians than to take
refuge with the Roman Empire*[2]. But these occurrences
happened soon after 435, for in the first letter Nestorius
mentions the synod of Ephesus as a fact of the recent
past. Scholars therefore could suppose and actually

---

[1] Evagrius, h. e. 1, 7, pp. 14–16; *Nestoriana*, pp. 198–201.

[2] ἵνα μὴ πάσαις ἐκ τούτου γενεαῖς τραγῳδῆται κρεῖττον εἶναι βαρβάρων
αἰχμάλωτον ἢ πρόσφυγα βασιλείας ῥωμαϊκῆς (Evagrius, 1, 7, p. 15, 12 f.;
Nestoriana, p. 199, 12 ff.).

did suppose that death soon put an end to the sufferings of the banished Nestorius. He feels himself an old man even as early as the time of these letters.

But now the *Treatise of Heraclides* teaches us that Nestorius was still alive at least in the autumn of 450, for the news of the death of the Emperor Theodosius, who died 28 July 450, had penetrated even to the loneliness of his exile. Professor Bethune-Baker[1] goes even further, thinking—in my opinion without sufficient grounds—that Nestorius must have died after the council of Chalcedon, about 452. During at least 15 to 16 years, therefore, Nestorius endured the hardships of exile. How many sufferings these years may have seen! Nestorius does not speak much of them. But he remarks incidentally, that *for many years he never had a moment of repose or any human comfort*[2]. Surely the person claims our interest who in spite of all this could write[3]: *The goal of my earnest wish, then, is that God may be blessed on earth as in heaven. But as for Nestorius,—let him be anathema! Only let them say of God what I pray that they should say. I am prepared to endure and to suffer all for Him. And would God that all men by anathematizing me might attain to a reconciliation with God.*

[1] *Nestorius and his teaching*, pp. 34–37, and *Journal of theol. studies*, IX, 1908, pp. 601–605.

[2] Bedjan, p. 519; Nau, p. 330.

[3] Bedjan, p. 507 f.; Nau, p. 323.

Thus, if we are interested by what the *Treatise of Heraclides* teaches us about the life of Nestorius, in no less a degree ought our interest to be awakened by what we learn about his doctrine.

As early as about 440 Socrates the church-historian defended, with the impartiality which distinguished him, his contemporary Nestorius against the grave misrepresentation to which his doctrine was exposed. People, as he says[1], thought that Nestorius regarded the Lord as a mere human being, as did Paul of Samosata and Photinus. *But*, so he continues[2], *I read his writings and I will say the truth : he did not hold the same opinions as Paul of Samosata and Photinus nor did he at all regard the Lord as a mere man, only he abhorred the term θεοτόκος as a bugbear.*

In a still higher degree Luther did justice to Nestorius. In his book *Von Conciliis und Kirchen* he confesses that he himself for some time did not understand what the error of Nestorius was, and that he also thought that Nestorius had held Christ to be nothing more than a man, as the popish decrees and all popish writers declared; but that after having looked more accurately at the accounts he saw that this was false[3]. This, too, according to Luther, was wrongly assumed about Nestorius, that he made two persons of the one Christ. *Nestorius,* Luther says, *really does not teach more*

---

[1] h. e. 7, 32, 6.   [2] l.c. 8.

[3] *Erlanger Ausgabe, Deutsche Schriften*, 2. Aufl. 25, 364.

*than one Christ; hence he could not regard Christ as two
persons; otherwise he would have said a Yes and a No
in the same article, contradicting himself*[1]. Nestorius,
he says[2], rightly believed that Christ was God begotten
of the Father from all eternity and man born of Mary
the Virgin; and, he declares[3], it was right, too, that
Mary did not bear the Godhead. But Luther thought
that Nestorius as *a rough and unlearned man* did not
comprehend the *communicatio idiomatum*, which in his
opinion justifies the phrase that God was born of Mary,
just as a mother (although the soul of her child does
not come from her) is nevertheless not only the mother
of the body, but the mother of the child[4].

Luther had but a very limited knowledge about
Nestorius. To the increased knowledge of our day
even before the discovery of the *Treatise of Heraclides*
the doctrine of Nestorius showed itself in a still more
favourable light. As early as ten years ago I wrote in
the *Realencyklopädie für protestantische Theologie und
Kirche: If Nestorius had lived in the time of the council
of Chalcedon, he would possibly have become a pillar
of orthodoxy*[5]. Now the *Treatise of Heraclides* teaches
us that Nestorius lived roughly speaking till the time of
that council. Accurately speaking there is no trace of the
Chalcedonian synod in the *Treatise of Heraclides*, and
the passages which seem to point to the time following it

[1] l.c. p. 365. [2] l.c. p. 366. [3] l.c. p. 367.
[4] l.c. p. 367. [5] xiii, 741, 15 f.

must in my opinion be explained otherwise[1]. Hence
I believe that the monophysitic stories asserting that
Nestorius had been invited to the council of Chalcedon,
but died a dreadful death on the journey thither[2] are
right in so far that Nestorius did not live to see the
opening of the council in October 451. But he saw the
beginning of the reaction which followed the so-called
robber-synod of Ephesus in 449. He even read the
famous letter of Pope Leo to Flavian of Constantinople,
which was of such decisive importance for the determina-
tion of Chalcedon and was acknowledged as a norm of
doctrine by this council. What was his judgment about
this letter of Leo's? Many times in the *Treatise of
Heraclides* he declares that Leo and Flavian taught
the truth and that their opinion was exactly the same
as his[3]. He even tells that he was begged by friends to
write to Leo of Rome, but he did not do it, lest—so he
says—through the prejudice existing against him he
should hinder him (*i.e.* Leo) who was running a right
course[4].

Because of all this, Professor Bethune-Baker, in
his above-mentioned book, *Nestorius and his teaching,*

[1] Comp. Hauck's *Real-Encyklopädie*, xxiv, 241, 36 ff.

[2] Comp. F. Nau, *Nestorius d'après les sources orientales*, Paris,
1911, p. 51 ff.; Evagrius, h. e. 2, 2, ed. Bidez and Parmentier,
p. 39, 17 ff.

[3] Bedjan, pp. 466, 474, 495, 514, 519; Nau, pp. 298, 303, 316,
327, 330.

[4] Bedjan, p. 519; Nau, p. 330.

thought he could maintain on the ground of the *Treatise of Heraclides* that Nestorius was not a Nestorian but was perfectly orthodox[1]. This thesis and the *Treatise of Heraclides* on which it is based are indeed both able to awaken our interest in Nestorius.

And still a third factor capable of arousing our interest besides my *Nestoriana* and the *Treatise of Heraclides* must be named. The French translator of the *Treatise of Heraclides*, F. Nau, has added to his translation four further almost new Nestoriana. He thinks he has discovered the original Greek text of three sermons of Nestorius on the story of the temptation, of which I knew only fragments from the first and third[2]. I had grounds for supposing that more of these sermons existed in manuscripts of Chrysostomus, but I did not succeed in finding such material[3]. The new discovery, I fear, is looked upon in a too optimistic manner by its editor. The new sermons certainly contain actual sections of homilies of Nestorius; but taken as a whole they do not seem to me to be of a really different kind from that Pseudo-Chrysostomus-homily from which I took the fragments of the sermons on the story of the temptation. Hence I cannot believe that the new sermons present the homilies of Nestorius on the temptation in an unaltered and complete form[4].

[1] pp. vii and 197 ff.
[2] Nau, pp. 333–358; *Nestoriana*, pp. 341–347.
[3] *Nestoriana*, p. 149.
[4] Comp. Hauck's *Real-Encyklopädie*, xxiv, 242, 29 ff.

More interesting, therefore, in my opinion, is the
fourth *Ineditum* which Nau gives in a French translation, after a Syrian British Museum manuscript to which
I pointed in my *Nestoriana*[1]. I refer to a fragment
of a letter of Nestorius to the inhabitants of Constantinople, the beginning and end of which were previously
known by a quotation made by the Monophysite
Philoxenus of Mabug[2]. I did not include this letter
in my *Nestoriana*, because with all other scholars I
regarded it as a monophysitic forgery intended to
discredit the doctrine of Pope Leo by showing it to be
approved by Nestorius. Indeed the letter appears for
the first time in monophysitic circles—in the writings
of Philoxenus about 520[2] and, what escaped the notice
of Nau, about 570 in the so-called anonymous *Historia
miscellanea*[3]. But according to the Syrian translator[4]
the Nestorians also, *e.g.* Simon Bar Tabbahê about 750[5];
acknowledged it as genuine, and since we know from
the *Treatise of Heraclides* the judgment of Nestorius
about Flavian and Leo there is no longer a plausible
objection which may be raised from this side against
the genuineness of the letter. I confess, however, that
I am not rid of all doubts. Certainly a definite judgment
is not possible till the whole of the letter be brought to

[1] p. 84.   [2] Comp. *Nestoriana*, p. 70.

[3] *Die Kirchengeschichte des Zacharias Rhetor in deutscher Über-
setzung* von K. Ahrens und G. Krüger, Leipzig, 1899, pp. 23, 31 ff.

[4] Nau, p. 376.

[5] Assemani, *Bibliotheca orientales*, III, 215.

light; for now between the beginning quoted by
Philoxenus and the fragment of the British Museum
a section is missing, the length of which we do not know.
Nevertheless the genuineness of the letter seems to me
now to be more probable than the contrary[1].

The beginning of the letter refers to the synod of
Constantinople, held in 448 by Flavian for the purpose
of condemning Eutyches, and the criticism of his
doctrine given by Leo in his letter to Flavian. *It is
my doctrine,* so Nestorius declares, *which Leo and
Flavian are upholding*[2]. Then, after the omissions, some
assertions corresponding to the doctrine of Nestorius only
as described by Cyril, are disproved. Then follow
polemics against Cyril, rejecting various quotations from
the Fathers which he was in the habit of using in
supporting his doctrine, these quotations being for the
most part apollinaristic forgeries[3]. Then the letter
ends in exhortations. These conclude with the words
preserved also by Philoxenus: *Believe as our holy
comrades in the faith, Leo and Flavian! Pray that
a general council be gathered in order that my doctrine,
i.e. the doctrine of all orthodox Christians, be confirmed.
My hope is, that when the first has taken place, the
second, too, will come to pass*[4]. Here Nestorius is
wooing the interest of his readers for the council of

[1] Comp. note 3.   [2] Nau, p. 374; I, 3.
[3] This fact evidently is in favour of the genuineness of the letter.
[4] Nau, p. 375; III, 19.

Chalcedon before it was held. Was his doctrine really in harmony with that of this council ? Was this heretic a rudely maltreated exponent of orthodoxy ?

These questions, you see, are not only raised by Professor Bethune-Baker; but we, too, have to raise them, when we are considering the material we find in the sources.

Hence I hope that, while dealing with these questions, I shall succeed in gaining your further interest during the course of the next three lectures.

In the next lecture we shall see that really to no other heretic has been done such great injustice as to Nestorius. The last two lectures will deal with the doctrine of Nestorius and his position in the history of dogma.

II

In the preceding lecture we saw that by the increased knowledge of the works of Nestorius and especially by his lately rediscovered *Treatise of Heraclides*, written not long before his death, and by his still later letter to the inhabitants of Constantinople, the question is raised whether this heretic was a rudely maltreated exponent of orthodoxy.

About his doctrine we shall speak in the next lecture, to-day it will only occasionally be mentioned. For what now will occupy us is the fact that he was

indeed so rudely maltreated that his life really became
what he himself called it—a *tragedy*.   This tragedy is
composed of five acts : first the undivided affection of his
parish was robbed from him, then the sympathies of the
Occident, then the favour of the court and his episcopal
office ; then he was brought into disfavour as a heretic
also amongst the majority of his friends, and finally as
an exiled and forgotten man he was exposed to common
condemnation.

1

It is well known that Nestorius in April 428 was
called out of the monastery of Euprepios, in the neighbourhood of Antioch, to the vacant bishopric of Constantinople[1].   We knew before the discovery of the
Treatise of Heraclides that it was the aversion of the
court to the election of a Constantinopolitan which
caused the decision to be in his favour[2].   Now we are
told more about this by an address which Nestorius in
his *Treatise of Heraclides* puts into the mouth of the
Emperor Theodosius[3].   Of course this address cannot
be regarded as given by the Emperor in these very
words ; but it is certainly trustworthy in what it tells
about the events in Constantinople.   We see here that
the sentiment of the court was the result of lengthy

[1] Comp. Hauck's *Real-Encyklopädie*, XIII, 737, 45 ff.

[2] l.c. p. 737, 37 ff.

[3] Bedjan, p. 377 ff.; Nau, p. 242 ff.; comp. Bethune-Baker,
Nestorius and his teaching, p. 6 ff. note 3.

transactions, in which the emperor made great con-
cessions to the monkish party and its leader, the archi-
mandrite Dalmatius. The monks themselves, according
to the narration of Nestorius, finally asked for the
decision of the court[1]. They, too,—later the most
embittered enemies of Nestorius—had at first no ground
for being discontented with his election. And, apart
from the heretical parties, which experienced the anti-
heretical zeal of the new bishop soon after his enthrone-
ment[2], this contentment was at first general[3].

But already before the end of Nestorius' first year
of office, the controversy began. Nestorius asserts in
the *Treatise of Heraclides* in just the same manner as
in a letter of December 430 to John of Antioch and in
his *Tragedy*, that he was not its beginner—he had
found a quarrel over the question as to whether Mary
was to be called θεοτόκος or ἀνθρωποτόκος, when he
arrived at Constantinople, and in order to settle it, he
had suggested the term χριστοτόκος[4]. When did
Nestorius do this? I think it was common opinion that
it took place in his "first sermon on the θεοτόκος," which
dates perhaps as far back as 428, perhaps only from the
beginning of 429. But in the fragments of this sermon[5]

---

[1] Bedjan, p. 379; Nau, p. 243 f.; Bethune-Baker, p. 8, note.

[2] Comp. Hauck's *Real-Encyklopädie*, xiii, 738, 1 ff.

[3] l.c. p. 737, 53 ff.

[4] Bedjan, p. 151; Nau, p. 91; ep. ad Joann., *Nestoriana*,
p. 185, Tragoedia, *Nestoriana*, p. 203.

[5] *Nestoriana*, pp. 249–264; comp. pp. 134–146.

the term χριστοτόκος does not occur. Now Nestorius
in his *Treatise of Heraclides* tells us that the quarrelling
parties, which abusively designated each other by the
names of "Manicheans" and "Photinians", came into the
bishop's palace and begged his counsel. He recognised
that neither the friends of the θεοτόκος were Manicheans
nor were the upholders of the term ἀνθρωποτόκος
adherents of the heresy of Photinus, and he declared
that both terms, when rightly understood, were not
heretical, but as a safer one he suggested the term
χριστοτόκος[1]. In this way, Nestorius narrates, the
parties were reconciled, and they were at peace with
one another until Cyril of Alexandria intruded himself
in the matter[2].

In this account, three points are worthy of consideration. First the notice that Nestorius advised the
quarrelling parties in his home. This report is undoubtedly trustworthy, for in his first sermon on the
θεοτόκος Nestorius directly makes mention of such
persons, who shortly before in his presence argued
against each other the question whether Mary should be
called θεοτόκος or ἀνθρωποτόκος[3]. This extension of
our knowledge as regards the place where Nestorius
advised the contending parties seems to be very unimportant. But that this is not the case we shall now

[1] Bedjan, p. 151 f.; Nau, p. 91 f.   [2] l.c. pp. 152 and 92.
[3] *Nestoriana*, p. 251, 21 ff.: *Audiant haec, qui..., sicut modo
cognovimus, in (ex?) nobis invicem frequenter sciscitantur : θεοτόκος...
Maria, an autem ἀνθρωποτόκος ?*

see, if we discuss the second point which in the above-
quoted narration of the *Treatise of Heraclides* seems to
be worthy of consideration.

Nestorius, as I mentioned, says here he had declared
that both terms, θεοτόκος as well as ἀνθρωποτόκος, rightly
understood, were not heretical, but that he recommended
as more safe the term χριστοτόκος[1]. This account of
Nestorius seems to be untrustworthy; for his well-known
first sermon on the θεοτόκος, preserved in long fragments[2], seems wholly to exclude the term θεοτόκος; and
it is likewise well known that Nestorius was continually
reproached for interdicting or at least refusing to give
to Mary the title θεοτόκος[3]. Even his afterwards
unfaithful friend, John of Antioch, asked him in a letter
of the autumn of 430 to give up his opposition against
this designation of Mary[4]. Is Nestorius, therefore,
telling a falsehood when he narrates that he had
declared the θεοτόκος, when rightly understood, to be
non-heretical? Here the place of meeting between
Nestorius and the quarrelling parties becomes important.
For, while I do not believe that Nestorius even in his
first sermon on the θεοτόκος, in spite of his criticism,
declared the term to be nevertheless tolerable, yet it is
not quite improbable that he did so previously in the

[1] Comp. above, p. 29.

[2] Comp. above, p. 28, note 5.

[3] Comp. sermo 18, *Nestoriana*, p. 300, 15: *Non dicit, inquiunt,
τὸ θεοτόκος, et hoc est totum, quod nostris sensibus ab illis opponitur.*

[4] Mansi, IV, 1065 B.

presence of the contending parties. This would agree
with what he narrated as early as December 430 in his
answer to the above-mentioned letter of John of Antioch[1].
And even in his first letter to Pope Celestine, after
having expressed his strong aversion to the term
θεοτόκος, he nevertheless wrote: *The term may be
tolerated*[2]. Hence we can give credit to the statement
of Nestorius, that from the beginning he did not regard
as intolerable the term θεοτόκος if rightly understood.
His position was this: he feared the term would originate
false ideas[3], and for this reason and because he believed
the term unknown to the orthodox Fathers of the past,
he had nothing in its favour and undoubtedly opposed it
on frequent occasions; but even in a sermon of the spring
of 429, which was known to Cyril before writing his
epistola dogmatica, he declared: *If you will use the
term θεοτόκος with simple faith, it is not my custom to
grudge it you*[4]. Afterwards in a sermon, which cannot
be dated, but was certainly delivered before the spring
of 430, he was able to say: *I have already repeatedly
declared that if any one of you or any one else be simple
and has a preference for the term θεοτόκος, then I have*

[1] *Nestoriana*, p. 185, 10 f.: *volentibus concessi, ut pie genitricen vel
particen dei virginem nominarent.*

[2] l.c. p. 167, 24: *ferri tamen potest hoc vocabulum.*

[3] Sermo 10, *Nestoriana*, p. 273, 4 f.: τὴν τῆς λέξεως προφορὰν
ἀσφαλίζομαι, τὸν ἐν τῇ λέξει κρυπτόμενον κίνδυνον ὑφορώμενος.

[4] l.c. p. 272, 13 f.: εἰ μετὰ πίστεως ἁπλῆς τὸ "θεοτόκος" προέφερες,
οὐκ ἄν σοι τῆς λέξεως ἐφθόνησα.

nothing to say against it—only do not make a Goddess of the virgin[1]. And even before the letter of John of Antioch mentioned above Nestorius came to an understanding with his clergy about the necessary use and meaning of the term θεοτόκος[2].

How under these circumstances was such a passionate controversy as that which followed, possible? What was it that deprived Nestorius of the undivided affection of his parish which he enjoyed at the beginning?

First it may be noted that the enemies of Nestorius were persuaded that bad heresies lurked behind his opposition to the term θεοτόκος. As early as the spring of 429 Eusebius, afterwards bishop of Dorylaeum, accused Nestorius by means of a public placard of thinking as Paul of Samosata[3]. Even at that time Nestorius was reproached for regarding Jesus as a mere man[4]. This reproach however was still more groundless than the indignation about his opposition to the term θεοτόκος. Hence this reproach, too, cannot be the first and the true cause of the controversy.

Nestorius declares in the above-quoted passage of the *Treatise of Heraclides*—and this is the third point

[1] *Nestoriana*, p. 353, 17 ff.: Εἶπον δὲ ἤδη πλειστάκις, ὅτι εἴ τις ἢ ἐν ὑμῖν ἀφελέστερος, εἴτε ἐν ἄλλοις τισὶ χαίρει τῇ τοῦ " θεοτόκος " φωνῇ, ἐμοὶ πρὸς τὴν φωνὴν φθόνος οὐκ ἔστι. μόνον μὴ ποιείτω τὴν παρθένον θεάν.

[2] ep. ad Joann. *Nestoriana*, p. 184, 21 ff.

[3] Mansi, IV, 1008 E-1012 B (Greek text) and V, 492-494 (Latin text); comp. *Nestoriana*, p. 49.

[4] *Nestoriana*, p. 259, 16; 284, 2; 285, 12.

which in his statement needs explanation—that the real
cause of the controversy is to be found in the intrigues
of Cyril of Alexandria[1]. These intrigues on their part,
according to what Nestorius tells in the continuation of
the above-quoted passage[2], originated in accusations
which were brought against Cyril himself. Cyril is
regarded by Nestorius as having framed the dogmatic
controversy for no other reason than to keep these
accusations in the background. Nestorius raised this
reproach against Cyril as early as in the late summer
of 430 in a letter to the bishop of Rome[3]; and that this
reproach was well grounded, I tried to show as far back
as 1903 by pointing to a letter, written by Cyril to his
clerical agents in Constantinople[4]. After long explanations about the perverted doctrine of Nestorius he says
in this letter: *I had till now no quarrel with him and
wish him betterment; but for supporting my enemies he
shall give answer before God. No wonder if the dirtiest
persons of the city, Chairemon, Victor and others, speak
ill of me. May he, who incites them, learn that I have
no fears about a journey or about answering them.
Often the providence of the Saviour brings it about that
little things cause a synod to be held, through which His
church is purified. But even if others and honourable
men should accuse me on his instigation—that wretched*

---

[1] Comp. above, p. 29.   [2] Bedjan, p. 152 f.; Nau, p. 92.

[3] ep. ad Caelest. 3, *Nestoriana*, p. 181, 10 f.

[4] Hauck's *Real-Encyklopädie*, xiii, 745, 30 ff.; comp. 743, 28 ff.

*man shall not hope that he can be my judge. I will
withstand him, if I come thither, and it is he who shall
answer for error*[1]. Nevertheless Cyril says in a
following section of this letter preserved only in its Latin
text : *If he professes the right faith, then shall be made
the most perfect and firmest peace. If he longs for that,
let him compose an orthodox confession of faith and send it
to Alexandria....Then I, too,...will publish a writing and
declare that nobody shall reproach one of my fellow-bishops
because his words—so I shall say—are rightly meant*[2].
Does not this mean: If he does what I wish (pointing
naturally and especially to the accusations, mention of
which is cleverly omitted), then he is no heretic ! To
give you a full idea of the plottings of Cyril as shown
by his communication with his agents I must add a
further quotation from the letter which occupies us. It
is out of the last part of the Greek text which by ancient
scholars[3] was held to be a supplement to the letter.

---

[1] Cyril, *ep.* 10, Migne, ser. graeca, 77, p. 65 D ; comp. the Latin
translation of Marius Mercator, ed. Baluze, p. 106 = Migne, l.c.
p. 74 f. It is noteworthy that Marius Mercator, a partisan of Cyril,
suppressed the words ὁ δείλαιος [μὴ προσδοκάτω]; he translates : *Non
igitur speret*, etc. Veracity was not a common virtue among the
Christians of that time !

[2] ed. Baluze, p. 108 = Migne, l.c. p. 77 f.: *Si rectam fidem profi-
teatur, fiet plenaria et firmissima pax. Quam si in voto gerit, scribat
catholicam fidem et mittat Alexandriam. Si haec ex affectu cordis
intimi scribantur, paratus sum et ego pro viribus meis similia scribere
et edere ac dicere, nullum debere gravari consacerdotum meorum, quia
ejus voces, dicimus, habent intentionem ac propositum manifestum.*

[3] Garnier in his edition of Marius Mercator, 1673, II, 56 = Migne,

Cyril says here[1]: *I received and read the petition you sent me, which, after having received my consent, is purposed for presentation to the Emperor. But since it contains various complaints against my brother there —or what shall I call him[2]?—I kept it back for the time, lest he should reproach you saying: you accused me as a heretic before the Emperor. But I composed another petition, in which I declined to be judged by him, pointing to his enmity and proposing that ...the judgment be handed over to other officials. Read this petition and present it, if need be. And if you see that he continues to scheme against me and really tries to set all things against me, write it to me at once. Then I shall choose some wary and prudent men and send them as soon as possible. For, as it is written[3], I will not give sleep to mine eyes or slumber to mine eyelids till I have finished the fight for the salvation of all.*

Whoever knows this advice of Cyril to his agents cannot doubt that the accusations brought against Cyril played a prominent rôle in the beginnings of the Nestorian controversy, and will, therefore, put confidence in what Nestorius tells about this matter in his *Treatise of Heraclides*. The agents of Cyril, he narrates[4],

l.c. p. 78; Tillemont, *Mémoires*, ed. of Venice, xiv, 755; Ch. W. F. Walch, *Historie der Kezereien*, v, 392, note 4.

[1] Migne, l.c. p. 68 c–69 a.
[2] κατὰ τοῦ ἐκεῖσε—ἢ ἀδελφοῦ ἢ πῶς ἂν εἴποιμι;
[3] Psalm 132, 4.
[4] Bedjan, p. 152 ff.; Nau, p. 92 f.

counselled the contending parties not to accept the
term χριστοτόκος. They schemed, agitated and were
to be found everywhere, referring always to Cyril as
their ally. Then, according to Nestorius' narration,
men who had complaints against Cyril, brought speakable
and unspeakable things against him before the Emperor
and requested at the same time that Nestorius should
be judge. Nestorius then sent for Cyril's clerical agents
and asked them to explain the situation. *But these,* to
use Nestorius' own words, *were annoyed and said to me :
What, you admit an accusation against the patriarch of
Alexandria and do not at once condemn the accusers as
calumniators without trial ?...We contest your right and
with good ground ; for that would be a dangerous en-
couragement of accusers, while it will be a profit to you to
keep him* (Cyril) *as your good friend and not to turn him,
who is famous because of his importance and who is among
the great, into an enemy. Then I answered them : I have
no desire for a friendship which would make me guilty
of injustice, but only for such which without respect of
persons does God's work. Thereupon they returned :
We will report it to the patriarch. Since that time,*
continues Nestorius, *he became my irreconcilable enemy
and ready for anything. He started a quarrel in order
to decline my judgment on account of my enmity, and to
outwit his accusers according to his custom, and to keep
the charges, brought against him, in the background.
This he managed to do, and then presented a petition*

asking that the judgment might be handed over to others[1].
As evidence of this, Nestorius quoted the above-
mentioned[2] conclusion of (or supplement to) Cyril's
letter to his agents, adding a sharp criticism.

We do not know which were the charges made
against Cyril before the emperor and before Nestorius
—they do not seem to have been of a dogmatic kind;
but, in my opinion, nobody can rightly dispute that
they were of decisive importance for the dogmatic
accusations which Cyril brought against Nestorius.

There is, however, one argument which could perhaps
be advanced against this. Hefele, the Roman Catholic
author of a famous history of the councils, objected[3]
that Cyril did not speak of the fact that his name was
slandered by false accusers before his second letter to
Nestorius, the so-called *epistola dogmatica*[4], which was
written about the end of January 430, while even
his first letter[5] to Nestorius contained the dogmatic
charges against him. The observation seems at first
to be right. For Cyril's letter to his agents, which we
have discussed, is contemporary with his *epistola
dogmatica* to Nestorius[6], in spite of the differing tone of
the two letters[7]. Nevertheless Cyril spoke of his being

[1] Bedjan, p. 153 f.; Nau, p. 93.　　　　[2] p. 35.

[3] Cf. J. v. Hefele, *Conciliengeschichte*, 2nd ed. II, 165 f.

[4] *ep.* 4, Migne, 77, 44–49.　　[5] *ep.* 2, Migne, 77, 40 f.

[6] Garnier, *opp. Marii Mercatoris*, II, 53.

[7] Comp. *ep.* 4, Migne, 77, p. 48 D: ταῦτα καὶ νῦν ἐξ ἀγάπης τῆς
ἐν Χριστῷ γράφω παρακαλῶν ὡς ἀδελφὸν κ.τ.λ.; *ep.* 10, p. 68 A: μὴ

accused before his second letter to Nestorius and the
contemporary letter to his agents. We learn this from
the *Treatise of Heraclides*. We saw[1] that Nestorius
here quoted and discussed the last part of Cyril's letter
to his agents, which by ancient scholars was held to be
a supplement to it; and the French translator of the
Treatise of Heraclides really is of the opinion that
Nestorius quoted only the mere conclusion of this letter[2].
But in no words of Nestorius is there a hint that he
deals with a part of a letter[3]. And more: if he had
known the beautiful phrase which we found in a
preceding section of the letter: *That wretched man
shall not hope that he can be my judge* etc.[4], he would
not have passed it by. Hence he knew the "supplement"
as a separate letter. That it really was one[5] is
confirmed by the translation of the letter to the agents
made by Cyril's contemporary Marius Mercator; for in
this translation the "supplement" is missing[6]. Then

προσδοκάτω δὲ ὁ δείλαιος, ὅτι κ.τ.λ.; and 68 c: κατὰ τοῦ ἐκεῖσε—ἢ
ἀδελφοῦ ἢ πῶς ἂν εἴποιμι; κ.τ.λ.

[1] Above, p. 34 f.   [2] Nau, p. 93, note 6.

[3] Nestorius however omitted at least an introductory sentence; for
the opening words of the "supplement": Τὸ δέ γε σχεδάριον κ.τ.λ.
cannot have been the exordium of a letter.

[4] Above, p. 34, note 1.

[5] Comp. the restriction made above in note 3.

[6] Baluze, p. 108. Garnier (II, 56), giving Peltan's (comp.
Nestoriana, p. 9 f.) Latin translation by the side of the Greek text,
has induced some of his readers (*e.g.* Walch, *Historie der Kezereien*,
v, 392, note 4, and, as it seems, also Migne, ser. gr. 77, p. 78) to take
the Latin text as a translation of Mercator.

the question arises as to when the "supplement-letter,"
so to speak, was written, and this question must be
answered by the assertion that it was earlier than the
letter to the agents as the conclusion of which it is
found in the Greek manuscripts[1]. For in the supplement-
letter, Cyril, even writing to his own agents, is not yet
sure whether he shall call Nestorius a brother or not,
and he will not yet give Nestorius cause for the reproach
that his agents denounced him as a heretic. The
supplement-letter is written, therefore, at least as early
as the first letter of Cyril to Nestorius, dating from
about late summer 429. Nestorius in his *Treatise of
Heraclides* seems to regard it as still earlier, for his

[1] About these manuscripts comp. *Nestoriana*, p. 8 ff. In the
manuscripts used by Peltan in his translation (comp. *Sacrosancti...
concilii Ephesini acta omnia Theodori Peltani...opera...latinitate
donata*, Ingolstadt, 1576, p. 220) and by the *editio Commeliana* (Τὰ
πρακτικὰ τῆς οἰκουμενικῆς τρίτης συνόδου κ.τ.λ., 1591, p. 73), in the cod.
Coislin. 32 (*saec.* XIII) of which Professor Henry Lebègue, of
Paris, kindly has sent me a collation, in the codices Monacenses 115
and 116 (both *saec.* XVI; *Nestoriana*, p. 10, I gave erroneously the
numbers 114 and 115) about which I received kind information from
the Royal Library of Munich, and in the cod. Vat. 830 (*saec.* XV), as
I learnt from a kind letter of Dr Erich Katterfeld, now at Rome,
the "supplement" (τὸ δέ γε σχεδάριον κ.τ.λ.) immediately follows
the preceding sentence (explicit: εἰ μή τις γένηται μετάγνωσις). But
the Greek text given by these manuscripts proves itself to be very
badly preserved, as is shown even by the address (πρὸς τοὺς Κων-
σταντινουπόλεως κληρικοὺς στασιάζοντας); the Greek manuscripts
cannot therefore give evidence against the hypothesis that the
"supplement" originally was a separate letter or part of such.
The Latin versions of the *Acta Ephesina* do not contain Cyril's letter
to his agents (comp. Mansi, v, 465 ff.).

narration gives the impression that the conversation
between him and Cyril's agents took place some time
before he received the first letter from Cyril[1]. There
are arguments against asserting that Nestorius was
right in presuming this. I shall not lay any stress
upon the fact that, according to Cyril's letter to pope
Celestine[2], it was only the doctrine of Nestorius which
gave him offence; for we have ground to distrust this
holy man. And also the objection that the affair of
the accusations against Cyril probably did not last a
whole year or more, is not decisive. But it is certain
that a reason for opposing the doctrine of Nestorius was
to be found by Cyril in the party-difference between
the Alexandrian and the Antiochian schools and in the
rivalry between the sees of Alexandria and Constantinople. Cyril's letter to the Egyptian monks in
which, about Easter 429, without mentioning Nestorius,
he began to oppose his doctrine, really may have been
brought forth by the party-difference alone. In Constantinople, too, in the very beginnings of Nestorius'
time as bishop, there certainly were theologians and
laymen who opposed his teaching for no other reason
than because they were adherents of a different theological tradition. I leave, therefore, the question
undecided as to whether the supplement-letter of Cyril
to his agents was earlier than his first letter to Nestorius

[1] Comp. Bedjan, p. 157; Nau, p. 95.
[2] *ep.* 11, Migne, p. 89 ff.

or not. But it is certain that Cyril, who before writing his *epistola dogmatica* had knowledge of a sermon of Nestorius in which he allowed the use of the term θεοτόκος[1], could have come to an agreement with him as easily as with the Antiochians afterwards in 433[2], if he had not had, on account of the charges brought against himself, an interest in discrediting him. More than the heretic Nestorius, the "Saint" but really very unsaintly Cyril is to be held responsible for the Nestorian controversy. And it is not improbable that his agents in Constantinople were among those and behind those who aroused the first opposition against the teaching of Nestorius.

Nestorius was not quite guiltless, as he had been incautious in his polemics against the θεοτόκος. But it seems not to have been his fault that he made an enemy of Cyril. He, Cyril, the Saint, had the chief part in bringing it about that Nestorius lost the common confidence of his parish.

2

And Cyril did more. At about the same time that he wrote his *epistola dogmatica* he prepared for war against Nestorius. He composed his five books

---

[1] sermo 10, *Nestoriana*, pp. 265–277, which contains the passage quoted above, p. 31, note 4, is mentioned in Cyril's letter to his agents (*Nestoriana*, p. 264, 7) and this letter is contemporary with the *epistola dogmatica* (comp. above, p. 37, note 6).

[2] Comp. below, p. 53 f.

adversus Nestorium[1], a work which opposed and denounced as heretical 43 quotations from the sermons of Nestorius, which partly he had previously adapted to suit his polemical ends[2]. Then he sent this work, translated into Latin, to the bishop of Rome together with a letter as untrue as it was clever[3]. About the same time he wrote three doctrinal letters really against Nestorius, but without mentioning his name, and addressed these to the emperor, to the empress and to the sister of the emperor, the "*Augusta*" Pulcheria[4]. With the first of these actions which opens the second act of our tragedy Cyril was astonishingly fortunate. I say *astonishingly fortunate*, for it is a riddle that Rome, whose dogmatic traditions were nearer to those of the Antiochians than to those of Cyril, let herself be guided by Cyril. In order to explain this riddle we can point to the fact that Rome had taken it amiss of Nestorius that he had received in Constantinople some banished western adherents of Pelagius[5]. One could even say that Rome took up her position against

---

[1] ed. Pusey, Oxford, 1875.

[2] Comp. Nestorius, tragoedia, *Nestoriana*, p. 205 ff. and *liber Heracl.* Nau, p. 222, note 2.   [3] *ep.* 11, Migne, pp. 80–89.

[4] Mansi, iv, 617–679; 679–802; 803–884=Migne, ser. graec. 76, 1133–1200; 1201–1336; 1336–1420; comp. Theodosius, *ad Cyrillum*, Mansi, iv, 1109 D, E.

[5] Comp. Marius Merc. *exemplum commonitorii*, ed. Baluze, p. 132 f.; Nestorius, *ad Caelestium* (*Nestoriana*, p. 172 f.) and *ad Caelestinum, ep.* 1 (*ibid.* p. 165); Caelestin. *ad Nestorium*, Mansi, iv, 1034 B.

Nestorius before Cyril's action. For the seven books
of Johannes Cassianus *contra Nestorium*, the writing
of which was instigated by Rome, show no influence of
the material sent by Cyril, as they deal only with
three of the earliest Constantinopolitan sermons of
Nestorius, evidently sent by Nestorius himself together
with his first letter to pope Celestine[1]. But the work
of Cassianus itself is a riddle. Is it not monstrous to
build up a strongly antinestorian work on this small
basis of three sermons? This piece of monstrous daring
cannot be explained unless it be that Rome was
prejudiced against Nestorius. Is the reception of the
Pelagians in Constantinople a sufficient ground for this
prejudice? Hardly. For as regards these Pelagians
Nestorius demanded advice of the Roman bishop in his
very first letter[2]. He would doubtless have sent them
away if the pope had asked this. But Celestine of
Rome had left unanswered at least three letters of
Nestorius. The reason he afterwards gave, viz. that the
letters of Nestorius had first to be translated into Latin[3],
deserves to be met by us with an incredulous shake
of the head. Was the real reason perhaps plottings of
Cyril? Cyril declares in May 430, in a letter to the
pope, that he had not written before to any of his
fellow-bishops about Nestorius[4]. As regarding the

[1] Comp. *Nestoriana*, pp. 51 f., 57, 156–158.

[2] *Nestoriana*, p. 166, 9 ff.

[3] *ad Nestor.* Mansi, IV, 1026 D.

[4] *ep.* 11, 1, Migne, 77, 80 C.

pope this must be true. But Cyril may have had his
confidents also in Rome;—I believe him to have been
capable of the most reckless intrigues. Indeed he says
in the conclusion of his above-discussed supplement-
letter to his agents: *The necessary letters will soon be
written to the necessary persons*[1]. However it may
have been, at any rate it must be charged to Cyril
that Celestine of Rome came to the firm conviction
that Nestorius was a heretic. And in an astonishing
degree the pope's actions followed the advice of Cyril.
In a synod at Rome he condemned Nestorius and notified
this, the 11th of August 430, to Cyril, to Nestorius,
to John of Antioch and others, to whom he had been
advised to write by Cyril[2]. The letter to Nestorius
was sent to Cyril for forwarding; it declared that
Nestorius was to be regarded as excommunicated, if he
did not recant within 10 days[3]. It is well known that
Cyril made the best of the success he had had at
Rome: he held a synod in Alexandria and wrote in its
name his third letter to Nestorius, the so-called
epistola synodica, which ends in the famous 12
anathematisms which Nestorius was to accept within
10 days on penalty of excommunication[4]. It was
Sunday, the 6th of December 430, when this letter of

[1] *ep.* 10, Migne, 77, p. 69 A.

[2] Mansi, IV, 1018 ff.; comp. the marginal note, p. 1050 D and
Cyril, *ep.* 11, 7 (*ad Caelest.*), Migne, 77, 85 A.

[3] Mansi, IV, 1035 A B.

[4] *ep.* 17, Migne, 77, 105–121.

Cyril together with that of the pope was delivered to
Nestorius by an Alexandrian legation[1]. Now there
was an enmity not only between Nestorius and Cyril
and his adherents, but also between him and the
western division of the church.

Nestorius was not quite guiltless as regards this
course of events. His behaviour towards the Pelagians
had not been cautious, and the tone of his letters had
perhaps displeased the pope. But it was tragic that
there was a Cyril who was capable of turning the
mistrust of Nestorius which previously existed in Rome
into enmity.

3

In this case we find the turning point, as is usual,
in the third act. The emperor, in spite of (or rather
because of) the above-mentioned letters of Cyril, remained at first still inclined towards Nestorius[2]. For it
was Nestorius and no other who succeeded in inducing
the emperor to call a new ecumenical synod[3]. On the
19th of November 430 the emperor ordered that it
should be gathered together in Ephesus on Whitsunday
next, *i.e.* the 7th of June 431[4]. To Cyril it was notified

[1] *Nestoriana*, p. 297, 25.

[2] Comp. Theodosius, *ad Cyrillum*, Mansi, IV, 1109 ff.

[3] Comp. above, pp. 5 and 12, and Nestorius, *ad Caelest. ep.* 3
(*Nestoriana*, p. 182, 12).

[4] Mansi, IV, 1111 ff.; Easter-day fell in 431, according to the
Alexandrian Easter cycle, on the 19th of April (comp. E. Schwartz,
Christliche und jüdische Ostertafeln, *Abhandlungen der Konigl. Gesell-
schaft der Wissenschaften zu Göttingen*, Neue Folge, VIII, 6, 1905, p. 48).

also by a very ungracious imperial letter, which in the strongest terms required his appearance before this synodical court[1]. Under these circumstances Nestorius could, on the 6th of December 430, receive with perfect composure the letters from Rome and Alexandria. The council would examine the matter, as he believed; and he looked forward to it without any fear. For he was convinced of the orthodoxy of his teaching, and the emperor was favourably inclined toward him; Cyril, on the contrary, was under suspicion for his doings and, as Nestorius with many others thought, also for his doctrine, and was out of favour with the emperor[2].

But Cyril was clever enough to change his position in Ephesus from that of anvil to that of hammer. Three things enabled him to do so. Firstly the great number of Egyptian bishops he had brought with him, secondly the support he found in Memnon the bishop of Ephesus and so in the population of that city, thirdly the effrontery with which he, who as having been accused ought to have remained in the background, pushed himself forward into a leading position[3]. Before the Antiochian bishops and the Roman legates had arrived he and his adherents opened the council on the 22nd of June[4], though 15 days after the appointed

[1] Mansi, IV, 1109 f., comp. especially, p. 1112 c.
[2] Comp. his sermon of December 12th, *Nestoriana*, p. 299, 25 ff.
[3] Comp. *liber Heraclidis*, Bedjan, p. 256 f.; Nau, p. 155.
[4] X Cal. Jul., Mansi, IV, 1123 and V, 772 A.

time[1], nevertheless in an arbitrary manner. John of Antioch had, in a still existing letter written on the journey, given a prospect of his and his countrymen's arrival within 5 to 6 days[2], and this letter had arrived at Ephesus at the latest on the 20th of June[3]; 68 bishops on the 21st of June had protested against the opening of the synod before the arrival of the Antiochians[4], and the commissioner, whom the emperor had sent to Ephesus, the count Candidian, emphatically demanded that the opening should be postponed[5]. But Cyril could not be hindered from making the best of the favourable situation. That Nestorius did not present himself before this party-council is comprehensible. They condemned him then *in absentia*[6] and incited the people of Ephesus to tumultuous approbation of this judgment[7]. At the latest four days

---

[1] Comp. above, p. 45, note 4; Memnon (Mansi, IV, 1129 D) counts 16 days, including the first and the last day.

[2] Mansi, IV, 1121.

[3] John's friends declared June 21st (comp. the next note): *juxta quae nuper suis litteris intimavit* (Mansi, V, 765 c). Cyril's lost letter to John of the 20th of June (Mansi, IV, 1272 c) seems to have been an answer to John's letter.

[4] Mansi, V, 765–768 (*directa pridie quam celebrarentur gesta contra Nestorium*, i.e. XI Cal. Jul.= June 21; comp. Mansi, V, 765, note d).

[5] Comp. his *contestatio* of June 22nd: *haec non semel sed saepius admonens...nihil profeci* (Mansi, V, 771 c).

[6] Mansi, IV, 1211. It was in the first session of the Cyrillian council (June 22nd).

[7] Mansi, IV, 1264 A B; comp. *Nestoriana*, 188, 19 ff.

after the opening of the Cyrillian council the Antiochians arrived[1], and, as they, too, on the 26th of June[2],
probably the very day of their arrival[3], opened with
Nestorius and others the council or rather their party-
council, and deposed Cyril and Memnon, there was,
therefore, then, one party-council standing in opposition
to the other. The Roman legates who arrived last of
all joined the Cyrillian synod.

Now it was for the emperor to decide. After many
transactions, which need not be described, induced by
the demonstrating monks of Constantinople, he heard
delegates of both parties[4], and if not earlier at least
then ceased to be a protector of Nestorius. Nestorius
himself made this easier for the emperor by writing
to Constantinople that he, if the right doctrine were
sanctioned, would willingly renounce his bishopric and
return to his monastery at Antioch[5]. Nevertheless the

---

[1] Hefele, 2nd ed. II, 192, note 2 (1875), left it undecided whether
John arrived June 26th or the 27th; but even before the publication
of the *Bibliotheca Casinensis*, I, 2, p. 24 (published 1873), it was to be
seen in Mansi, v, 773 B, that the first session of the Antiochian
council was held the 26th of June (VI Cal. Jul.).

[2] Comp. the preceding note.

[3] This is pretended by the Cyrillian party (Mansi, IV, 1333 B);
and the notice in the Synodicon (Mansi, v, 773 A; *Bibliotheca
Casin.* I, 1, p. 58 A): *mox enim post triduum veniens Joannes*, probably
confirms it, since the preceding document dates from June 23rd
(Mansi, v, 772 C: *hesterno die*).

[4] Hefele, II, 213 ff., 230 ff.; comp. now Nestorius, *liber Heraclidis*, Bedjan, p. 375 ff.; Nau, p. 241 ff.

[5] *Nestoriana*, p. 194, 16 ff.; comp. p. 195, note = Mansi, v, 792 f.

emperor when at about the end of July[1] he sent to
Ephesus a second commissioner, the count John, one
of his confidants, was not yet on Cyril's side: the royal
order delivered by count John confirmed all three de-
positions, that of Nestorius, of Cyril and of Memnon[2],
and when John committed all three into close custody, he
consigned Nestorius to the care of count Candidianus,
who was inclined towards him, while Cyril seems to have
been treated in a less friendly manner[3]. The question
of the doctrine was regarded by the court as still open;
and as count John was not able to bring the parties at
Ephesus to an understanding with one another, in the
second half of August[4] delegates of each group were
called to the capital, or rather to the neighbouring city
of Chalcedon, for further negotiations. But as regards
the persons one decision was given just at this time:
the emperor resolved about the end of August[5] to send

[1] Hefele, II, 219, note 2.   [2] Mansi, IV, 1395 f.

[3] Mansi, IV, 1398 B = V, 780 E; comp. *Liber Heraclidis*, Bedjan,
p. 387 f.; Nau, p. 248 f.

[4] A letter written by the Antiochian delegates immediately after
their arrival at Chalcedon dates from *Gorpiaei mensis undecimo*,
(Mansi, V, 794 B = IV, 1406 E), i.e. according to Tillemont (edition of
Venice, XIV, 776 f) the 4th or the 11th of September: and although
each of these dates seems to me open to controversy (comp. Pauly's
Real-Encyclopädie, 2nd edition, VII, 1664), we can and must let the
matter rest. Nearly the same time, as given by both dates, is
indicated by the course of events.

[5] Eight days before the letter mentioned in the preceding note was
written (Mansi, V, 794 A).—The Alexandrian report in Mansi, V,
255 and 658 f., connecting the imperial order regarding Nestorius—

back Nestorius into his monastery. This resolve which was followed, though perhaps not instantly[1], by the return of Nestorius to Antioch, seemed regrettable to all Antiochians[2], but corresponded, as we saw, to the request of Nestorius. The emperor, however, did not order this because Nestorius had wished it. Nestorius was now in open disfavour; not even his name could be mentioned before the emperor[3]. But as for Cyril the situation had changed in his favour: he had been able to escape from custody and to return to Alexandria[4], and as

erroneously styling it an order of *banishment*—with the election of Maximian, which happened a month later, is not trustworthy (comp. Tillemont, xiv, 777 a).

[1] Nestorius, *ep.* 10 (*Nestoriana*, p. 195 f. = Mansi, v, 793), and the *epistola praefecti*, answered by this letter, seem to indicate a delay, and the Antiochians as late as in their answer to the second letter of their delegates (for the heading of chapter xxvi in Mansi, v, 794, belongs to chapter xxviii, comp. *Bibliotheca Casinensis*, i, 1, p. 60) apparently did not know anything about the departure of Nestorius, for they wrote only: *ea vero, quae contra personam, quae injustitiam pertulit, facta sunt, cognoscentes, totius obstuporis sumus taciturnitate perculsi* (Mansi, v, 796 B).

[2] Comp. *epist. legat. orient.*, Mansi, v, 794 A B : *...imperatori placuerit, dominum Nestorium ab Epheso dimitti, quocumque ire voluerit. Et omnino doluit anima nostra, quia, si hoc verum est, ea, quae absque judicio et illicite facta sunt, interim roborari videntur.*

[3] Comp. *Theodoreti ep. ad Alex. Hieropol.*, Mansi, v, 800 B, and *epistola legatorum orientalium*, Mansi, iv, 1420 E (=v, 802 A).

[4] That Cyril escaped from custody is told not only by Acacius of Beroea (Mansi, v, 819 c: *dum custodiretur in Epheso, fuga est usus*) and by Nestorius (*Liber Heraclidis*, Bedjan, p. 388; Nau, p. 249: *Cyrille...échappa à ceux qui le gardaient..., et gagna sa ville*); also the postscript given to the *ultima sacra imperatoris ad synodum* (Mansi, iv, 1465; v, 805) in the Synodicon (Mansi, v, 805) says:

successor to Nestorius a man was elected, Maximian by name, with whom he could be quite satisfied[1]. And when the emperor, though no decision had been reached at Chalcedon, officially dissolved the council, Cyril's return to Alexandria was allowed and Memnon was permitted to remain in his office at Ephesus[2].

This change of feeling in the court is explained by Nestorius in a passage of his *Treatise of Heraclides* by the fact, as he thinks, that Cyril gave or promised much money to the count John and through him to the emperor[3]. He presumes, that the favour which John showed towards him was as unreal as his disfavour towards Cyril, as this disfavour only enabled him to let Cyril escape from custody[4]. The narration by which Nestorius tries to prove this assertion[5] is very similar

missa sacra ultima omnium, directa est, quando jam redierat in civitatem suam beatus Cyrillus. Now this *sacra* was later than the consecration of Maximian which took place on the 25th of October (Socrates, 7, 37, 19; Mansi, v, 255 B=659 A: *post hoc*): the Alexandrian deputies of the Ephesian synod assisted at this consecration (Mansi, v, 255=658; Cyril, *ep.* 32, Migne, 77, 157 f. = Mansi, v, 265), and the Antiochian deputies, too, had not yet departed from Chalcedon, although they were not allowed to assist at Maximian's consecration (Acacius Beroe., Mansi, v, 819 CD). But Cyril arrived at Alexandria as early as October 30th (Mansi, v, 255 C=659 A); hence he left Ephesus before the council was dissolved.

[1] Comp. Cyril, *ep.* 32 (Migne, 77, 157 f.; Mansi, v, 265)

[2] Mansi, IV, 1765 B; v, 805 B.

[3] Bedjan, p. 385 ff.; Nau, p. 247 ff.

[4] Bedjan, p. 388; Nau, p. 249.

[5] Bedjan, p. 385; Nau, p. 247 f.

to that which we find in a letter of Acacius of Beroea, written as early as 431[1]. But in this letter it is the eunuch Scholasticus, not count John, who is bribed, and other differences, too, are to be observed. We see, therefore, that Nestorius is repeating party-gossip. Nevertheless there may be a foundation of truth in this gossip, for Nestorius and the Antiochians complain again and again—and, as we shall see, not without grounds—of the briberies of Cyril. In another place in his *Treatise of Heraclides* Nestorius tells us, that the *Augusta* Pulcheria supported Cyril, because he, Nestorius, offended her by not paying her, on account of doubts about her virtue, the ceremonial honours which she as a virgin demanded[2]; and in this narration the disfavour, which Nestorius had experienced at the hands of Pulcheria, cannot be an invention of the writer. Then it is interesting to note that Cyril in the beginnings of the controversy tried, as we saw[3], to win Pulcheria to his cause, and afterwards, as we shall see[4], sought her favour even by means of presents. But the endeavours of Cyril to gain favour with Pulcheria are only one example of his intrigues. More generally speaking it can be said: it was essentially Cyril's work, that the council of Ephesus, demanded by Nestorius

[1] *ad Alexandr. Hierop.*, Mansi, v, 819 c.

[2] Bedjan, p. 148; Nau, p. 89; comp. *ep. ad Cosmam*, Nau, p. 363, 8.

[3] Above, p. 42.

[4] Below, p. 55, note 3.

himself and hailed by him with joy, led to the result that Nestorius lost the emperor's favour and his bishopric. It was the tragedy of Nestorius' life, that, in Ephesus, the question was whether he should be overthrown or Cyril, a man as unscrupulous as he was greedy of power.

4

After the transactions at Ephesus the tragedy of Nestorius' life came to its end in two acts, the first of which is now to be treated. I say *after the transactions at Ephesus* and not *after the council of Ephesus*, for "a council of Ephesus," an ecumenical council of Ephesus, never existed. Two party-councils had sat and cursed each other; the dogmatic question had remained undecided. The Antiochians continued to hold Nestorius in esteem and to treat as heretical the anathematisms of Cyril; the latter, for his part, regarded Nestorius as a condemned heretic and had grounds for thinking that his council had proved his anathematisms[1]. The church of the East was divided. The emperor, assisted by Maximian, the new bishop of Constantinople, forced the parties to a peace by means of the union of 433. The document of this union between Cyril and the Antiochians is Cyril's *epistola ad orientales*[2], in which he accepted an Antiochian confession of faith,

[1] Comp. Tillemont, *Mémoires*, edition of Venice, xiv, 398 and p. 758 (note 26).

[2] *ep.* 39, Migne, 77, 173–181.

composed in 431 at Ephesus, probably by Theodoret.
The prolonged transactions which led to this union are
even in their details sufficiently known to us. But
I am glad not to have to treat them now; for the
Treatise of Heraclides, although very often dealing with
this union, adds nothing to our knowledge here, as far
as I have been able to see.

I remark only, that Nestorius in his *Treatise of
Heraclides* gives a sharp and right characterisation
of the situation which preceded the union[1]. Cyril
and John of Antioch had each two wishes in the event
of peace. Cyril wished to see acknowledged, firstly his
council and the condemnation of Nestorius, secondly
his anathematisms; John on the other side wished as
ardently that the first should not take place and
secondly, that Cyril should recant his anathematisms.
Cyril, in order to retain his power, let himself be
bartered down to a great extent. He accepted the
Antiochian confession of faith and was contented with
the fact that his anathematisms were not condemned.
But he did not give up the demand, that his council
should be acknowledged and Nestorius be anathematised.
He again set in play all his possible means for attaining
this end. And here we are in a position to follow
his actions by means of documents, which show clearly
that he did not even hold himself back from bribery.
These documents are a letter of Cyril's archdeacon

[1] Bedjan, pp. 395–403; Nau, pp. 254–259.

Epiphanius to Maximian of Constantinople[1], and, supplementing it, a list of the presents which Cyril at the same time sent to Constantinople[2]. I regret that time forbids me to quote this letter, but I beg every one who holds my judgment upon Cyril to be too harsh, to begin his study on the holiness of this man by reading this letter[3]. The aim of Cyril's intrigues and briberies

[1] Mansi, v, 987–989.

[2] *Bibliotheca Casinensis*, I, 2 (*Florilegium Casinense*), p. 46 f., comp. I, 1, p. 72.

[3] Now in the printed text I am able to add some quotations, Mansi, v, 988 D:...*Nunc igitur, domine mi sanctissime, impone tibi omne in hac causa studium. Scriptum est a domino meo, fratre vestro, et dominae ancillae dei reverentissimae Pulcheriae et praeposito Paulo et Romano, cubiculario, et dominae Marcellae, cubiculariae, et dominae Droseriae, et directae sunt benedictiones dignae eis. Et ei, qui contra ecclesiam est, Chrysoreti praeposito, magnificentissimus Aristolaus paratus est scribere de nonnullis, quae angelus tuus* (read: *sanctitas tua* = ἡ σὴ ἁγιότης? comp. Mansi, note i) *debeat impetrare; et ipsi vero dignae transmissae sunt eulogiae* (comp. in the list of presents, *Bibl. Cas.* I, 2, p. 47 a: *Praeposito Chrysoreti, ut nos impugnare desinat, coacti sumus duplicia destinare*). *Scripsit autem dominus meus, frater vester, et domino Scholastico* (comp. *Bibl. Cas.* l.c. p. 47 b, and above, p. 52) *et magnificentissimo Arthebae, ut ipsi conveniant et persuadeant Chrysoreti tandem desistere ab oppugnatione ecclesiae; et ipsis vero benedictiones dignae directae sunt. Festina igitur et tu ipse, sanctissime, supplicare dominae ancillae dei Pulcheriae Augustae, ut iterum ponat animam suam pro Domino Christo—puto enim, quod nunc non satis curet pro sanctissimo vestro fratre Cyrillo ut et omnes, qui sunt in palatio regis, et quicquid* (read: *quod aliquid?*) *avaritiae eorum deest, quanquam non desint et ipsi diversae benedictiones—, ut scribat increpative Joanni, quo nec memoria illius impii* (viz. *Nestorii) fiat. Scribatur vero et magnificentissimo Aristolao, ut instet ei* (viz. *Joanni) celeriter. Et roga dominam Olympiadem, ut*

shown by this letter was, that John of Antioch and his friends should be made willing to accept the judgment of his synod against Nestorius. John of Antioch yielded to Cyril at this point: to bring about the union he payed the heavy price of giving up his old friend. The same price was paid by almost all Antiochians who accepted the union, only Theodoret and a few others being excused from doing so.

From that time forth one could speak in ecclesiastical phraseology of *the holy ecumenical council of Ephesus*, which had condemned Nestorius. Nestorius could have accepted the confession of faith on which the union was based. It was, therefore, really tragic that the anathema against him was the price of the peace. He was now also robbed of his former friends, and there cannot be the least doubt that for this painful experience, too, he had to thank Saint Cyril.

et ipsa coadjuvet nos et ut insuper roget M a r c e l l a m et D r o s e r i a m, quia satis eam patienter auscultant...Et dominum meum sanctissimum Dalmatium abbatem roga, ut et i m p e r a t o r i mandet, terribili eum conjuratione constringens, et ut cubicularios omnes ita constringat, ne illius (viz. Nestorii) memoria ulterius fiat, et sanctum E u t y c h e n, ut concertet pro nobis...Subjectus autem brevis (comp. above p. 55, note 2) ostendit, quibus hinc directae sint eulogiae, ut et ipse noveris, quantum pro tua sanctitate laboret Alexandrina ecclesia, q u a e t a n t a p r a e s t a t h i s q u i i l l i c s u n t; clerici enim, qui hic sunt, contristantur, quod ecclesia Alexandrina nudata sit hujus causa turbelae...De tua ecclesia praesta avaritiae quorum nosti, ne Alexandrinam ecclesiam contristent... Festinet autem sanctitas tua rogare dominam P u l c h e r i a m, ut faciat dominum L a u s u m intrare et praepositum fieri, ut Chrysoretis (comp. above) potentia dissolvatur et sic dogma nostrum roboretur.

5

The last act of our tragedy may be treated shortly, but it stretches over a much longer period than any of the others. It was opened by the banishment of Nestorius to Oasis in the year 435[1], and not until sixteen years later was it closed by Nestorius' death[2].

We have only two accounts which give us information as to how this banishment of Nestorius came about. Nestorius himself, as we learn from Evagrius, narrated that for four years he had enjoyed at Antioch various tokens of esteem, but had then been banished to Oasis by order of Theodosius[3]. Evagrius adds that Nestorius did not say how fitting a measure this was, for also in Antioch Nestorius had not ceased his blasphemy, with the result that even Bishop John complained about it, and Nestorius was condemned to permanent exile[4]. The Nestorian legend, too, tells us that Nestorius had lived four years in Antioch and that then John of Antioch had caused his banishment out of jealousy of his influence[5]. That the first part of this account goes back to Nestorius' own narration is made probable by its concurrence with the words of Nestorius in Evagrius. It is, therefore, probable that also the

---

[1] Comp. below, note 3.   [2] Comp. above, p. 19 and 22.

[3] Evagrius, *h. e.* 1, 7, ed. Bidez and Parmentier, p. 13, 12 ff.

[4] l. c. p. 13, 16 ff.

[5] M. Brière, *La légende syriaque de Nestorius* (*Revue de l'Orient chrétien*, 1910, p. 21; Nau, p. xxi, note 1).

account given about John of Antioch in both sources
is derived from Nestorius. His banishment according
to this account took place in the year 435[1]. In the
same year, on the 30th of July, Theodosius, the emperor,
issued an edict which ordered the impious books of the
detestable Nestorius against the orthodox piety and
against the decrees of the synod of Ephesus to be
burnt, and which gave the name of Simonians (that
of an ancient heretical party) to his adherents[2]. The
wording of this edict and the account of Evagrius that
Nestorius had not ceased his blasphemy in Antioch
could make possible the conjecture[3] that the banishment of Nestorius and this edict against his books were
caused by what he had written in Antioch, especially by
his *Tragedy* which dealt with the decrees of the synod
of Ephesus. But this conjecture has its difficulties[4].
We are, therefore, obliged to take the edict as referring
to the earlier books of Nestorius and the account
of Evagrius to spoken blasphemies. All the more
important in this connection must have been the in-
stigatory efforts of John of Antioch. Pope Celestine,
too, petitioned the emperor as early as 432 for the
exile of Nestorius[5], and Cyril was probably working with

---

[1] Four years after the synod of Ephesus, comp. above, p. 57, note 3.

[2] Mansi, v, 413 f.; *cod. Theodosianus*, 16, 5, 66.

[3] *Nestoriana*, p. 88.

[4] For according to Evagrius (l. c. p. 13, 15 f.) Nestorius mentioned
in his *Tragedy* his banishment to Oasis.

[5] Mansi, v, 271 B.

the same end in view. These latter are not much to be
blamed for this wish. It is not the same with John
of Antioch. He may have had, even if jealousy was
out of the question, many grounds for finding the stay
of Nestorius in Antioch disagreeable—his mere presence,
after the union, was a reproach to him—but he has
much impaired his good renown by this Judas-deed.
And for Nestorius it was the consummation of his
tragic fortune that his final banishment was caused by
his former friend.

How rich the years of exile were in tragic events
we have seen already in the first lecture[1]. I merely
remark here that Nestorius in these years was even
before his death a dead man for the world—I mean
the orthodox church. He now was nothing but the
condemned heretic, nothing but the cause of offence
thrust out from the people of God.

He was really not dead: he hailed with joy the
change of the situation after the robber-synod, hailed
with joy Leo's letter to Flavian, hailed with joy the
new council he saw in prospect[2]. He did not live to
experience the fact that this council, too, condemned
him and that also Theodoret, who even up to his death
held to him, was forced to consent to this condemnation[3]. With this the tragedy of Nestorius' life came
to an end. Now he was regarded by all in the church
as a cursed heretic; now for him came to pass what,

[1] Above, p. 17 f.   [2] Comp. above, p. 25 f.   [3] Mansi, vii, 188 f.

according to the edict of 435, was to be the fortune
of his adherents: he had not only supported the
punishment of being covered with ignominy during his
lifetime, but also after his death did not escape from
ignominy[1].

The orthodox saw in his sufferings nothing but a
just penalty: Nestorius himself called his life a tragedy.
I, too, used the same expression. But his life was a
tragedy only if he was guiltless. The question as to
whether he was guiltless shall occupy us in the next
two lectures.

III

In the last lecture we spoke about the tragedy
of the life of Nestorius. Was it really a *tragedy*? His
enemies regarded his sufferings as deserved punishment
for his impiety. Were they wrong? Was Nestorius
really the guiltless victim of a tragic fortune? He was.
It is this which I wish to prove in this and the next
lecture.

I do not mean that Nestorius was altogether guiltless
in his life's misfortune. He was incautious, passionate
and reckless, and this, as we saw in the preceding lecture,
was not without unfavourable influence upon the course

---

[1] Mansi, v, 413 B: μήτε ζῶντας τιμωρίας, μήτε θανόντας ἀτιμίας
ἐκτὸς ὑπάρχειν.

of events. But no hero of a tragedy is quite guiltless. And we Christians know that we all have the old Adam in us as long as we live.

Only by understanding the word "guiltless" in a broader sense I am able to say that Nestorius was guiltless. His guilt was very slight in comparison with the heavy weight of his sufferings.

Socrates, the church historian, regarded, as we saw[1], the dogmatic charges against Nestorius as essentially unfounded. He thought the fault of Nestorius was his lack of knowledge[2]. But I must decline to accept for Nestorius this *privilegium ignorantiae*. It is true that Nestorius at first did not know that the term θεοτόκος was used by some of the orthodox Fathers of the fourth century. But this lack of knowledge is not a sign of ignorance. I won't say that Nestorius was a learned man. Neither the fragments of his works nor his *Treatise of Heraclides* show patristic or philosophical erudition. But his education was not in any way a merely rhetorical one. The *Treatise of Heraclides* and many of the earlier known fragments of Nestorius prove that, in spite of some inaccuracies in his terminology[3], he was a theologian well educated in dogmatics.

Luther thought that, besides his want of learning, it was fatal for Nestorius that he was a boorish and proud

---

[1] Above, p. 20.
[2] *h. e.* 7, 32, 8: ἀγνοοῦντα ἐφευρίσκω τὸν ἄνδρα.
[3] Comp. below, p. 90, note 1.

man[1]. This judgment was based on a very insufficient knowledge of the sources. But it may give us occasion to enquire whether the personal character of Nestorius was the cause of his tragic fortune.

Nestorius was passionate and dogmatic. John of Antioch reminds him in a letter of a scene from their earlier life in common, which may prove this[2]. And even an account, which is friendly to Nestorius, tells about him, that he was lacking in courtesy and amiability[3]. This characteristic is really shown in his letters to Cyril. Also his letters to Rome are not exactly models of courtesy. And even from the pulpit he sometimes declaimed against his enemies in a rough and passionate manner[4].

The account, which denied him amiability, points in explanation of this characteristic to the fact that Nestorius, as a monk, had no experience of worldly affairs[5]. Indeed, it was an unpolished nature he showed. But the merits of this naturalness came out as clearly as the demerits. Even now we see something straight and open in the letters and in the polemics of Nestorius. And comparing his writings

---

[1] Comp. above, p. 21.   [2] Mansi, IV, 1064 D.

[3] *ep. ad Cosmam*, Nau, p. 364, 9: *C'était un homme excellent et jalousé, qui n'avait pas l'expérience des affaires du monde et qui manquait de ce qu'on appelle amabilité.*

[4] In a sermon (*Nestoriana*, p. 300) he addressed Cyril: *Quid perturbationes ferinis rugitibus adferre conaris?*

[5] Comp. above, note 3.

with those of Cyril, which overflow with so-called piety, and even with some of the letters of John of Antioch[1], we are agreeably impressed by observing that Nestorius did not wrap up his thoughts in pious phrases. It is also deserving of mention that Nestorius, where he had confidence, showed nothing of narrow-minded sensitiveness. His answer to the above-mentioned letter of John of Antioch is proof enough of this[2]. I think he was also sincere when he asked Cyril the reproachful question: *Why did you not write me a friendly letter and inform me of the troubles in Egypt, their cause and the manner of settling them,* instead of writing to the monks about my doctrine[3]?

And it would be quite wrong to presume that Nestorius had also in his intellect something rough and blunt. He is, on the contrary, acute in his thinking, not without ability in his polemics, and here and there, by the use of fitting images, he shows that he was capable of fine observation[4].

The reproach that he was proud is still less well grounded. He seems to have had an exalted idea of the bishop's position to which he was called[5]. This will

---

[1] Comp. *e.g.* his letter to Cyril, mentioned above p. 47, Mansi, IV, 1121.   [2] *ep.* VII, *Nestoriana*, pp. 163–186.

[3] *Liber Heraclidis*, Bedjan, p. 158 f.; Nau, p. 96.

[4] Comp. *Liber Heracl.*, Bedjan, p. 188, Nau, p. 113 (cuttle-fishes), B. p. 189=N. 114 (fights with children), p. 204=123 (timid dogs), p. 338=217 (drowsy men), p. 438=280 f. (wounded snakes).

[5] I do not point here to the famous apostrophe, which, according

explain why he wrote to the Roman bishop with a
self-conscious assurance and agreed without hesitation
to become the judge of Cyril. But this self-con-
sciousness of office was something other than pride
and greed of power and glory. This is convincingly
proved by the fact, that Nestorius himself offered the
emperor to return to his monastery[1]; and he did not
only offer this, but he proved by the deed, that he
easily gave up his episcopal honours[2]. One cannot call
him proud who regarded nothing more blissful than
the calm stillness of the monastery[3]. And when in his
exile he surrendered himself to the governor, as we
saw[4], he showed himself not only straightforward and
honest, but also proved that he did not set a high value
on himself and his life. Finally his remark that he did
not write to Leo of Rome lest he should bring him into
discredit[5], may be taken as proof that striving after
glory and honour and esteem was far from him.

May we now realise that, nevertheless, in the
personal character of Nestorius are to be found the
grounds for the tragic course of his life? It is intelligible

to Socrates (7, 29, 4 f.), he gave to the king in his first sermon at
Constantinople: Δός μοι, ὦ βασιλεῦ, καθαρὰν τὴν γῆν τῶν αἱρετικῶν,
κἀγώ σοι τὸν οὐρανὸν ἀντιδώσω. For here, I think, Nestorius is to
be assumed as having spoken in the name of God.

[1] Comp. above, p. 48.

[2] Comp. *ep.* ix, *Nestoriana*, p. 194, 14 f.: *a me, teste deo, episco-
palis honor facillime respuatur.*

[3] l.c. p. 194, 22.   [4] Above, p. 18.

[5] Above, p. 22.

that a man with such characteristics was not exactly
suited to the taste of the court and especially of the
circle of that most pious lady, the *Augusta* Pulcheria;
he was not cut out for a courtier. But even if the
ground of his misfortune were to be found here, his life
should nevertheless be called a tragedy, for his sufferings
would have been too harsh a punishment. We can,
however, hardly assume that the characteristics we
discussed were the cause of Nestorius' unhappy
fate. For he enjoyed the favour of the court as long
as he lived in Constantinople and even longer, and his
enemies never pretended, as far as I know, that his
guilt rested in his personal character.

His enemies condemned him for his teaching. It
is, therefore, his teaching that we must examine.

Nestorius was an Antiochian as regards his theological upbringing. I do not believe that he was a personal pupil of Theodore of Mopsuestia—the chronology
contradicts this, and there are no convincing arguments
for this assumption[1]. But that he was educated in the
traditions of the Antiochian school is without doubt.

The Antiochian Christology is most easily compre-
hended, if we contrast it with Apollinarism, condemned
by the church about fifty years before Nestorius became
bishop of Constantinople. Apollinaris of Laodicea is
well known to have taught that a real incarnation
and a real unity of the historical person of Christ was

[1] Comp. Walch, *Ketzerhistorie* v, 315 f.

only intelligible, if the Logos took on himself not a perfect man, that is body and animal soul and intellectual soul or intellect, but joined himself with a human body and a human soul in such a manner that he himself became the intellect, the moving principle, in the new and united being. This idea of a substantial unity between the *Logos* and the human nature which resulted in the new and composite nature of the incarnate *Logos* seemed to the Antiochians to do away with the true manhood of Christ and with the possibility of his moral development. They taught, therefore, that the divine and the human nature in Christ were to be regarded as perfect each in itself, a human free will, too, having to be assumed in Christ. To maintain this, they laid stress on the assertion that the two natures in Christ were not altered by their union as substances which are chemically combined. Hence they did not think the union to be a substantial one.

Before going further I will make a short remark about the term *nature*, deferring discussion of the term *substance* till later. I can do it by quoting Professor Bethune-Baker. For this scholar is right in saying that the term *nature* at that time meant all the attributes or characteristics attached to a substance and as a whole always associated with it[1]. Apollinaris saw in Christ but one substance, viz. the substance of

---

[1] Comp. Bethune-Baker, *Nestorius and his teaching*, p. 48.

the Logos, to which in addition to its own characteristics those of the imperfect human nature were attached.

Nestorius was as strong an opponent of this Apollinaristic doctrine as any other Antiochian. Regarding his zeal in opposing it, it is characteristic that he almost always named Apollinaris in the same breath with Arius and Eunomius or placed the Apollinarists and the Arians side by side[1]. He had a right to do so; for the Arians were the first who looked at the incarnation, like Apollinaris, in a—I do not say *serious*—but mythical light. The pre-existent son of God, so was their teaching, really changed into man, taking the body from the virgin as his body so that he himself became the soul of this body and the subject of all experiences which are told of Jesus: he hungered, suffered, died. Hence the Arian Eudoxius expressly said that there were not in Christ two natures, the whole being one combined nature[2]. Nestorius knew of course that Apollinaris, differing from the Arians, regarded the pre-existent Son of God, following the decree of the Nicene synod, as ὁμοούσιος τῷ πατρί, and, at least in the second period of his development,

[1] Comp. *Nestoriana*, p. 166, 19; 170, 30; 179, 4; 181, 18; 182, 8; 184, 15; 185, 12; 194, 16; 208, 16; 267, 16; 273, 6 f.; 300, 20; 301, 4. 5. 16; 305, 15 f.; 312, 7; *Liber Heracl.*, *e.g.* B. 252 = N. 152; B. 261 = N. 157.

[2] Hahn, *Bibliothek der Symbole und Glaubensregeln*, 3rd edition, Breslau, 1897, § 191 p. 262: οὐ δύο φύσεις, ἐπεὶ μὴ τέλειος ἦν ἄνθρωπος, ἀλλ' ἀντὶ ψυχῆς θεὸς ἐν σαρκί· μία τὸ ὅλον κατὰ σύνθεσιν φύσις. Comp. Nestorius, *Liber Her.* B. 12 = N. 6, 5.

conceded that this λόγος took on a human body with a
soul[1]; but he was right in minimising this difference.
Here and there, he argued, the peculiar human nature
of Christ became perfect only when the Logos was added
to it, neither here nor there is Christ a real man as we[2];
and with acute perception he brings to light the
weakness of Apollinaris' theory.   Even if, he says, the
incarnation was thought by Apollinaris to be a voluntary
action of the *Logos*, nevertheless as soon as the unity
between the *Logos* and the body with human soul
was perfected, the union was after the manner of a
substantial one, not voluntary : the *Logos* was forced
nolens volens to suffer what his body and soul suffered[3].
And a second difficulty, too, is seen by Nestorius,
a difficulty which afterwards gave trouble to the
scholastics.   If the Son, so Nestorius argues, was united
substantially with the human nature, the same must be
assumed also of the Father and the Holy Spirit because
of the unity of substance in the Godhead, but if the
Father and the Spirit had not, in the same measure as
the Son, partaken in the sufferings of the historic
Jesus, then the unity of substance with the Father and
the Spirit is taken from the Son[4].

But these difficulties of thinking are not the
chief stumbling-block for Nestorius as regards the

[1] *Liber Her.* B. 50=N. 31.
[2] l.c. B. 50 f., 52 ff. = N. 31, 32 ff.
[3] l.c. B. 55 f. = N. 35.   [4] l.c. B. 56, 58=N. 35, 36.

Apollinaristic teaching. The chief cause of offence for
him is, that the *Logos* appeared here as capable of
suffering and dying and, therefore, his divine nature as
altered in itself. In opposition to these thoughts
Nestorius held by the Antiochian doctrine, afterwards
also acknowledged by the council of Chalcedon, that
the two natures in Christ were each perfect in itself
and unaltered.

This was also conceded by Cyril. In his *epistola
dogmatica* to Nestorius he had written: *The natures
which are brought together into a true union are different,
but of the two there is one Christ and one son, the
difference of the natures not being destroyed by the
union*[1]; and in contradiction to Apollinaris he, too,
contended that the *Logos* took on a perfect human
nature, not only body and animal soul, but also an
intellectual soul or a human intellect[2]. Where then
was the difference between this Alexandrian exponent
of the two natures and Nestorius? Cyril's formula,
also in the quotation which I have given, was: *one
Christ out of both, out of two natures.* This formula is
at the first glance unintelligible, since Cyril would not
assert a mixture of the natures and, apart from some
incautious utterances[3], really did not do so; but it

---

[1] *ep.* 4 Migne, 77, 45 c: διάφοροι μὲν αἱ πρὸς ἑνότητα τὴν ἀληθωὴν
συναχθεῖσαι φύσεις· εἷς δὲ ἐξ ἀμφοτέρων Χριστὸς καὶ υἱός· οὐχ ὡς τὴν τῶν
φύσεων διαφορᾶς ἀνῃρημένης διὰ τὴν ἕνωσιν κ.τ.λ.   [2] l.c. p. 45 B.

[3] Comp. *e.g. de recta fide ad Theodos.* 40, Migne, 76, 1193 B:
'Ιησοῦς Χριστὸς...εἰς ἕν τι τὸ μεταξὺ συγκείμενος.

is explained in Cyril by another term, viz. that of
hypostatic union: Cyril teaches a ἕνωσις καθ' ὑπόστασιν.
Nestorius, on the contrary, protested against this phrase.
In his *Treatise of Heraclides* he deals much with the
question of this phrase and openly says that he did not
understand it then (when he first heard it) and did not
understand it now[1].

Indeed this term has its difficulties. If we wish
to comprehend in which sense Cyril made use of it
and Nestorius opposed it, we must, as Professor
Bethune-Baker rightly remarks[2], put out of the
question that meaning of the term which is taught by
the council of Chalcedon and adopted by the orthodoxy
of later times, for this meaning is a result of a
development, which was not yet completed when Cyril
and Nestorius wrote. Originally ὑπόστασις is a
synonym of οὐσία, if this latter is understood in the
sense of real being; both words then may be translated
by *substance*. As synonymous with οὐσία the term
ὑπόστασις appears in the Nicene creed, because the
Logos here is deduced ἐκ τῆς οὐσίας τοῦ πατρός and the
assertion is anathematised, that he was ἐξ ἑτέρας οὐσίας
ἢ ὑποστάσεως. And Athanasius said even about the
end of his life: ἡ ὑπόστασις οὐσία ἐστι καὶ οὐδὲν ἄλλο
σημαινόμενον ἔχει ἢ αὐτὸ τὸ ὄν[3]. Αὐτὸ τὸ ὄν, *the being
itself*—that is the meaning of ὑπόστασις. The term

---

[1] *Liber Her.* B. 228=N. 138.   [2] *Nestorius and his teaching*, p. 47.
[3] *ad Afros* 4, Migne, 26, 1036 B.

means[1] τὸ ὑποκείμενον, as Aristotle said, the ultimate
reality which is the bearer of all the attributes which
are called the *nature* of a thing, the *substance* in the
sense in which the earlier philosophy, that of the
middle ages included, made use of this term and which
was afterwards criticised by Locke and Hume. The
term οὐσία could also be used in a generic sense and
then received a meaning similar to *kind* or *nature*, but
ὑπόστασις means only that which οὐσία could mean
in addition to its other meaning, viz., a single and
really existing being, whether material or immaterial.

As regards the doctrine of the Trinity these two terms,
originally synonymous to some extent, were differen-
tiated: one spoke of μία οὐσία and τρεῖς ὑποστάσεις in
the Trinity; but, as Professor Bethune-Baker rightly
observed[2], there is not any clear evidence that a similar
usage, a similar differentiation between οὐσία and
ὑπόστασις, had been extended in the time of Cyril to
the christological problem. Hence in the discussion
between Cyril and Nestorius on the relation of the
Godhead and manhood in Christ the term ὑπόστασις
must be understood as essentially synonymous with
οὐσία. Now Nestorius, just as the earlier Antiochians,
believed that the natures of Christ, as both really
existing in him, had each their ὑπόστασις: he spoke
of two ὑποστάσεις with as little scruple as of two

[1] Comp. Bethune-Baker, l.c. p. 48 ff.
[2] l.c. p. 50.

72 THE DOCTRINE

natures in Christ[1]. Cyril, on the contrary, expressly
condemned the διαιρεῖν τὰς ὑποστάσεις ἐπὶ τοῦ ἑνὸς
Χριστοῦ[2], the ἕνωσις καθ' ὑπόστασιν excluded for him
the existence of two ὑποστάσεις in Christ. In explaining
this theory he is not always fortunate, and in his
terminology he is not always consistent. Professor
Bethune-Baker is right in saying: "His use of the
expression ἕνωσις φυσική gives strong support to the
view that he used the parallel expression ἕνωσις καθ'
ὑπόστασιν in the sense of *substantial* rather than in
the sense of *personal* oneness[3]." Nevertheless his real
theory is clearly to be perceived. The divine *Logos*,
he thinks, who naturally has his ὑπόστασις or is an
ὑπόστασις, remained the one and the same that he was
before the incarnation, also after having assumed
human nature. He took in his ὑπόστασις a human
body, soul and intellect as his own body, soul and
intellect, so that his human nature had, therefore, no
ὑπόστασις. Christ's human nature was, according to
Cyril, nothing more than all the human characteristics
taken as a whole, which the λόγος σεσαρκωμένος had
as such. It existed, so to speak, before the incarnation
as the nature or substance of the human race; but
after the incarnation, because of the ἕνωσις καθ'

[1] Comp. *e.g. Liber Her.* B. 291 = N. 184, B. 302 = N. 192, B. 305 =
N. 193: *On ne doit pas concevoir une essence sans hypostase, comme si
l'union avait eu lieu en une essence.*

[2] *ep.* 17, *anath.* 2, Migne, 77, 120 c.

[3] Bethune-Baker, l.c. p. 174.

ὑπόστασιν, it cannot be regarded apart from the ὑπόστασις of the *Logos*. That is meant by Cyril's ἐκ δύο φύσεων εἰς.

It is easy to perceive that this theory is not conceivable. If it meant that the *Logos* became man in the manner of a mythical metamorphosis, this would be, although a false, yet a somewhat intelligible theory, and I am convinced that thousands of Cyril's adherents took this to be the meaning of his theory, and that even in our day thousands of simple Christian people understand the incarnation in this mythical interpretation. Cyril, however, asserted that this was not his meaning. Then, as I said, his theory is not conceivable. For what is a nature which has no real existence of its own? Is then the *Logos* not thought of as suffering and dying, in spite of Cyril's protest? or can one speak of sufferings and death where there is no suffering or dying subject, but only an impersonal nature? And is it still possible to say that Christ was a man as we are, if the human nature existed in him only as assumed in the ὑπόστασις of the *Logos* and as having become *his* human nature? Nestorius is quite right in reproaching Cyril that his doctrine resulted in a suppression of the manhood of Christ, for, according to Cyril's doctrine, the human intellect of Christ cannot be realised as operating in him[1]. The Christ of Cyril, as

[1] *Liber Herac.* B. 341 = N. 218, comp. B. 295 = N. 187: *Qu'est ce que l'homme parfait qui n'agit pas et qui n'est pas mû selon la nature*

Nestorius rightly observed, did not think with the
intellect of manhood, but with the intellect of the
God-*Logos*; he did not feel by means of a human soul
but in unity with his Godhead etc.[1]

Nobody can doubt that the doctrine of the Antiochian
school, which Nestorius held, was a clearer one. Christ,
according to them, was really a man who thought and
felt as a man and had his bodily, intellectual and moral
development as other men. Nevertheless they asserted
that Christ was also perfect in his Godhead, as the
Logos is ὁμοούσιος τῷ πατρί. But they were blamed
by their opponents for not having brought these two
ideas to such an agreement, that the oneness of the
person of Christ became comprehensible. They were
said to have divided Christ into two persons and two
sons—the eternal son of God and the son of Mary,—
the first being son of God by nature and the other only
by adoption.

Nestorius, too, is reproached for this, but he again
and again protested against this reproach. Christ, as
he continually says, was *one*: *one* Christ, *one* son of God,
one Lord, *one* πρόσωπον[2]. Also in the *Treatise of
Heraclides* there are numerous explanations of this kind.
If you, so he says to Cyril, *understand by the* ἕνωσις

de l'homme? Il n'est homme que de nom, corps de nom, âme rationnelle
de nom, celui qui n'est pas mû selon la nature de son être, etc.

[1] l.c. B. 251 = N. 152.

[2] Comp. *Nestoriana* Index s.v. Christus (p. 397 *b*), κύριος (p. 402 *a*),
υἱός (p. 407 *a*), πρόσωπον (p. 405 *a*).

καθ' ὑπόστασιν the union in the *πρόσωπον* of *Christ*,
then I agree with you[1]. And with the formulas which
he saw proposed by Flavian of Constantinople[2] or found
in Leo's letter to Flavian[3] he showed himself well
contented[4].

Thus apologising for himself, Nestorius was not
fortunate in his own time but he is in our time. For
Professor Bethune-Baker has in his book on Nestorius
and his teaching a particular chapter with the heading:
"Two persons not the teaching of Nestorius[5]," and here
we find Professor Bethune-Baker asserting: "It is
impossible to doubt that Nestorius was clear in his own
mind that his doctrine of the incarnation safeguarded
absolutely the unity of the subject. He did not think
of two distinct persons joined together, but of a single
person, who combined in Himself the two distinct
substances, Godhead and manhood, with their characteristics (*natures*) complete and intact though united in
Him[6]." Of course Professor Bethune-Baker does not
fail to recognise that the use of the term *πρόσωπον* in
Nestorius is somewhat "puzzling[7]," but nevertheless,

---

[1] *Liber Heracl.* B. 229 = N. 138 (condensed translation).

[2] Comp. Hahn, *Bibliothek der Symbole*, 3rd edition, § 223, p. 321:
ἐν δύο φύσεσιν...ἐν μιᾷ ὑποστάσει καὶ ἐν ἐνὶ προσώπῳ ἕνα Χριστόν, ἕνα
υἱόν, ἕνα κύριον ὁμολογοῦμεν.

[3] Hahn, l.c. § 224, pp. 321–330; *unitas personae in utraque
natura intelligenda* (c. 5, p. 326).

[4] Comp. above, p. 22 and 25.

[5] pp. 82–100.   [6] l.c. p. 87.   [7] l.c. p. 97.

without much discussion of the term πρόσωπον—some remarks are given[1]—he arrives at the conclusion that Nestorius "used the term *person* (πρόσωπον) to express that in which both the Godhead and manhood of our Lord were one"[2]; and his final judgment is, that Nestorius, though not sharing the later orthodox phraseology which declares the human nature of the Lord impersonal in itself but personal in him only, nevertheless seems to have made an attempt to express the same conception in other terms[3].

Here, I am afraid, I cannot agree with Professor Bethune-Baker, however much I sympathise with him in his doing justice to the miserable exile of Oasis.

First, it must be emphasised that πρόσωπον is for Nestorius not the same as what we call *person*. For our notion of *person* the main thing is the oneness of the subject or of the internal self. We can, therefore, use the term *person* only for rational beings or at least those living beings, in which—as in the case of the higher animals—we see some analogy to human thinking, feeling and willing. For Nestorius, who in this respect was influenced by the manner of speaking common at that time, the main thing in his notion of πρόσωπον, according to the etymology of the word and to the earlier history of its meaning[4], was the external

[1] l.c. p. 97.   [2] l.c.   [3] l.c. p. 98.
[4] Comp. Siegmund Schlossmann, *Persona und Πρόσωπον im Recht und im christlichen Dogma*, Kiel and Leipsic, 1906, p. 11 ff.

undivided appearance[1]. He was, therefore, able to call a bishop preaching from the pulpit *the πρόσωπον of the church* (because the church appeared in him)[2] and to say that Christ had exhibited in himself *the πρόσωπον of the human nature as being sinless*[3]. In his opinion, I believe, everything had its πρόσωπον, that is its appearance, its kind of being seen and judged. In not a few places in Nestorius, it is true, the meaning of πρόσωπον coincides with our understanding of the term *person*, e.g. "Cyril's πρόσωπον"[4] means Cyril, "these πρόσωπα" means these persons[5], and εἶς καὶ ὁ αὐτός and ἓν πρόσωπον may be used alternately[6]. Nevertheless, before we go further, I must lay stress on the fact that the notion of πρόσωπον in Nestorius grew upon another soil and, therefore, had a wider application than our term *person*.

Coming now to the matter itself I must firstly remark that the places in which Nestorius, just as Theodore

[1] Comp. *Liber Heracl.* B. 89 = N. 58: *L'homme est reconnu en effet au πρόσωπον humain, c'est à dire à l'apparence du corps et à la forme ⟨du serviteur⟩*; comp. B. 31 ff. = N. 18 ff., where Nestorius is regarding a soldier's uniform as his πρόσωπον. This conception of πρόσωπον makes intelligible the phrasings we find B. 241 = N. 145 (*dans tout ce que le prosôpon comporte*) and B. 276 = N. 174 (*en tout ce qui forme le prosôpon*).

[2] *Nestoriana*, p. 332, 13.

[3] l.c. p. 239, 18f.: δείξας ἐν ἑαυτῷ τὸ τῆς φύσεως πρόσωπον ἁμαρτίας ἐλεύθερον.

[4] *Liber Heracl.* B. 195 = N. 117.

[5] l.c. B. 197 = N. 118.

[6] l.c. B. 323 = N. 206.

of Mopsuestia[1], speaks about two πρόσωπα in Christ,
viz. the πρόσωπον of the Godhead and the πρόσωπον
of the manhood, are more numerous[2] than Professor
Bethune-Baker's book[3] leads us to suppose. Nestorius
as an adherent of the Antiochian school could as little
realise a really existing nature without πρόσωπον as
without ὑπόστασις[4], for the whole of the characteristics
which make the nature must, in his opinion, as
necessarily have a form of appearance, *i.e.* a πρόσωπον,
as a real being by which they are borne, *i.e.* an
ὑπόστασις. One place in the *Treatise of Heraclides* is
very characteristic in this respect. Here Nestorius is
asking Cyril: *Which of the natures do you think is
without πρόσωπον, that of the Godhead or that of the
manhood? Then you will no longer be able to say that
the God-Logos was flesh and that the flesh was Son*[5].
That is: if you think the Godhead without πρόσωπον
then there will be lacking the form of appearance which
the manhood could take on, and if the manhood, then

---

[1] Comp. *de incarn.* ed. H. B. Swete, *Theodori episc. Mops. in
epistolas B. Pauli* etc., II, 299, 18 ff.: ὅταν μὲν γὰρ τὰς φύσεις διακρί-
νωμεν, τελείαν τὴν φύσιν τοῦ θεοῦ λόγου φαμὲν καὶ τέλειον τὸ πρόσωπον·
οὐδὲ γὰρ ἀπρόσωπον ἐστιν ὑπόστασιν εἰπεῖν· τελείαν δὲ καὶ τὴν τοῦ
ἀνθρώπου φύσιν καὶ τὸ πρόσωπον ὁμοίως. ὅταν δὲ ἐπὶ τὴν συνάφειαν
ἀπίδωμεν, ἓν πρόσωπον τότε φαμέν.

[2] *e.g.* B. 78=N. 50; B. 94=N. 61; B. 106=N. 69; B. 305=
N. 194: *les natures subsistent dans leurs prosôpons et dans leurs
natures*; B. 341=N. 218.

[3] p. 97 f.

[4] Comp. *Liber Heracl.* B. 316=N. 202: *pour ne pas faire…les
prosôpons sans hypostase.*   [5] B. 305=N. 194.

the form of appearance of the flesh which the *Logos* could take on.

Nevertheless the number of those places in which Nestorius asserts that there was *one πρόσωπον* in Christ is much greater than that of those in which he speaks about the *πρόσωπα* in Christ. The former are found in great number already in the earlier known fragments[1] and in a still greater in the *Treatise of Heraclides*[2]. This formula is to be held as characteristic of the teaching of Nestorius. He repeats again and again that the natures were united in the *one πρόσωπον* of Christ. But what does he understand by this?

At first we must answer: Nestorius has in his mind the undivided appearance of the historic Jesus Christ. For he says, very often, that *Christ is the one πρόσωπον of the union*[3]. And he argued with Cyril: *You start in your account with the creator of the natures and not with the πρόσωπον of the union*[4]. *It is not the*

---

[1] Comp. *Nestoriana*, Index, s.v. *πρόσωπον*, p. 405 *a*.

[2] Comp. Nau's translation, Index, s.v. prosôpon, p. 388 *b*.

[3] *e.g.* B. 212=N. 128: *C'est donc le Christ qui est le prosôpon de l'union*; B. 223=N. 134 f.: *le prosôpon d'union est le Christ*; B. 250= N. 151; B. 307=N. 195.

[4] B. 225=N. 136; comp. B. 255=N. 154: *Pourquoi donc m'avez-vous condamné? Parce que je lui ai reproché de...commencer par celui-ci (Dieu le Verbe) et de lui attribuer toutes les propriétés*, and B. 131= N. 85: *C'est pourquoi celui-là (Cyrille), dans l'incarnation, n'attribue rien à la conduite de l'homme, mais (tout) à Dieu le Verbe, en sorte qu'il s'est servi de la nature humaine pour sa propre conduite.*

*Logos who has become twofold¹; it is the one Lord Jesus
Christ who is twofold in his natures². In him are seen
all the characteristics of the God-Logos, who has a nature
eternal and unable to suffer and die, and also all those
of the manhood, that is a nature mortal, created and
able to suffer, and lastly those of the union and the
incarnation³.* To understand this idea of Nestorius all
thoughts of a substantial union ought to be dismissed.
A substantial union—so Nestorius argues—including a
confusion, a mixture, a natural composition, would
result in a new being⁴. Here the natures are unmixed:
the *Logos ὁμοούσιος τῷ πατρί* is bodyless⁵ and is
continually what he is in eternity with the Father⁶, being
without bound, without limit⁷, but the manhood has a
body, is mortal, limited etc.⁸ These different natures
are united not substantially but in the *πρόσωπον* of
the union⁹; and it is to be noticed, that for Nestorius
there is nothing singular in such a union in itself, that

¹ B. 213=N. 128; B. 215=N. 130; B. 248=N. 150; B. 296=
N. 188.
² B. 213=N. 128; *Nestoriana*, p. 283, 13; 341, 2.
³ B. 249 f.=N. 151.
⁴ B. 250 f.=N. 151; comp. B. 236=N. 142.
⁵ B. 70=N. 45.   ⁶ B. 265=N. 160.
⁷ B. 304=N. 193; comp. B. 239=N. 144.   ⁸ B. 265=N. 160.
⁹ *e.g.* B. 213=N. 129: *L'union est en effet dans le prosôpon, et non
dans la nature ni dans l'essence*; B. 230=N. 139: *C'est pourquoi je
crie avec insistance en tout lieu que ce n'est pas à la nature, mais au
prosôpon, qu'il faut rapporter ce qu'on dit sur la divinité ou sur
l'humanité.*

is apart from the very natures which are united here. *I know,* he says, *nothing which would suit a union of different natures except a single πρόσωπον by which and in which the natures are seen, while they are giving their characteristics to this πρόσωπον*[1].

For the detailed explanation of this thought an idea is important which Professor Bethune-Baker has already noted[2] in the *Treatise of Heraclides,* viz. the idea that in Christ *the manhood is the πρόσωπον of the Godhead, and the Godhead the πρόσωπον of the manhood*[3]. Reading Professor Bethune-Baker's book one could think that this idea appeared only once or at least seldom. Really, however, it recurs again and again[4]. It is the leading idea of Nestorius that the natures of Christ made reciprocate use of their πρόσωπα[5], the Godhead of the form of a servant, the manhood of the form of God[6]. In this sense in the one πρόσωπον of Christ, according to Nestorius, *a union of the πρόσωπα*

---

[1] B. 230 = N. 138 f.

[2] p. 97.   [3] B. 144 = N. 168.

[4] Comp. *e.g.* B. 78 ff. = N. 50 ff.; B. 289 = N. 183; B. 305 = N. 193 f.; B. 334 = N. 203, etc.

[5] Comp. *e.g.* B. 341 f. = N. 219: *Pour nous, dans les natures, nous disons un autre et un autre, et, dans l'union, un prosôpon pour l'usage de l'un avec l'autre (ou: pour leur usage mutuel)*; B. 289 = N. 183: *l'humanité utilisant le prosôpon de la divinité et la divinité le prosôpon de l'humanité*; B. 307 = N. 195: *Ils prennent le prosôpon l'un de l'autre*; B. 334 = N. 213: *Elles (les natures) se servent mutuellement de leurs prosôpons respectifs.*

[6] *e.g.* B. 81 = N. 52; B. 90 f. = N. 59; B. 241 = N. 145.

took place[1] so that *this is that and that is this*[2]. Professor Bethune-Baker, who did not enter into a discussion of the last quoted formulas, says in reference to the former (viz.: *The manhood is the πρόσωπον of the Godhead and the Godhead is the πρόσωπον of the manhood*[3]): "These words come near to eliminating 'personality,' as we understand it, altogether, or at all events they suggest the merging of one personality in the other, each in each. This in fact seems to be the meaning of Nestorius. He is in search of the real centre of union and he finds it here. He uses the term πρόσωπον to express that in which both the Godhead and manhood of our Lord were one, even while remaining distinct from one another, each retaining its own characteristics[4]." I think that Professor Bethune-Baker is here still striving to find a metaphysical centre of union. In my opinion the idea of Nestorius is most easily[5] understood by us, if we look at Philippians ii, 6 ff. The *form of a servant* and *the form*

---

[1] B. 305 = N. 193: *L'union des prosôpons a eu lieu en prosôpon.* Comp. B. 213 = N. 129: *L'union est en effet dans le prosôpon et non dans la nature*; B. 275 = N. 174: *Il n'y a pas un autre et un autre dans le prosôpon*; B. 281 = N. 177: *Nous ne disons pas un autre et un autre, car il n'y a qu'un seul prosôpon pour les deux natures.*

[2] B. 331 = N. 211: *C'est dans le prosôpon, qu'a eu lieu l'union, de sorte que celui-ci soit celui-là et celui-là, celui-ci.* These last words are to be found very often.

[3] Comp. p. 81 with note 3. Similar sentences recur again and again.   [4] p. 97.

[5] About the difficulties which remain see below, p. 90, note 1.

of God here spoken about do not, according to
Nestorius, succeed each other, they are co-existent, *i.e.*
the one Christ shows us as clearly the form of God as
the form of a servant, and it is once expressly said
by Nestorius that *the form is the* πρόσωπον[1]. The
statement, that the πρόσωπα interchange, means,
therefore, that the *Logos* shows himself in the form
of a servant and the man in the form of God, this one
by humbling himself, the other by being exalted[2], or
as Nestorius says[3] with Gregory of Nazianzen[4]: θεοῦ
μὲν ἐνανθρωπήσαντος, ἀνθρώπου δὲ θεωθέντος.

Let us examine these two thoughts further. First,
that the union takes place in the πρόσωπον of the man.

The *Logos* humbled himself in willing obedience
unto death, yea, the death of the cross, taking on the
πρόσωπον of the man, who suffered and died, as his
own πρόσωπον[5]. From the annunciation, the birth and
the manger till death[6] *he was found in outward being
as a man, without having the nature of a man; for he
did not take the nature but the form and appearance of*

---

[1] B. 244 = N. 147.

[2] B. 84 f. = N 54 f.; B. 244 = N. 147; B. 341 = N. 218.

[3] *e.g.* B. 280 = N. 177; B. 307 = N. 195; B. 315 = N. 201; B. 330 =
N. 210 f.; B. 332 = N. 212; B. 360 = N. 231.

[4] *ep.* 101, M i g n e, 37, 180 A.

[5] Comp. B. 84 f. = N. 55; comp. B. 131 = N. 85: *La forme de
Dieu était en apparence comme un homme.*

[6] B. 132 = N. 85; B. 118 = N. 76: *Parce qu'il était Dieu et im-
mortel, il a accepté dans son prosôpon—lui qui n'était pas coupable—
la mort, c'est à dire ce qui est mortel et capable de changement.*

a man as regards all which the πρόσωπον *includes*[1]. But how can the *Logos* himself have the form of a servant if he did not have the human nature? An answer may be found in the following words of Nestorius: *God the Logos is said to have become flesh and son of man as regards the form and the* πρόσωπον *of the flesh and of the man, of which he made use in order to make himself known to the world*[2]. *It was the flesh, in which he manifested himself, in which he taught, in which and through which he acted, and that not as being absent; he made use of His* πρόσωπον *in the flesh, because he wished that he himself might be the flesh and the flesh He himself*[3]. *God had a beginning and development by manifestation*[4]. Nestorius takes this so earnestly that he says: *Christ is also God and he is no other than God the Logos*[5].

The second side of the idea we are discussing, viz. that the manhood in Christ shows itself in the form of God, is already partly explained by the preceding quotations, as they assert that it was the *Logos* who was to be seen in the man. But we need to have a clearer understanding of this second side of the idea

[1] B. 241=N. 145; comp. B. 252=N. 152: *Un et le même (est le) prosôpon, mais (il n'en est pas de même pour) l'essence; car l'essence de la forme de Dieu et l'essence de la forme du serviteur demeurent;* and B. 262=N. 158: *Il a pris la forme du serviteur pour son prosôpon et non pour sa nature ou par changement d'essence.*

[2] B. 230=N. 139.   [3] B. 80=N. 51.

[4] B. 274=N. 173; comp. below, p. 85, note 6.

[5] B. 218=N. 132.

also. Because the *Logos* manifested himself in the form of servant, the man appeared in the form of God. *No one ever saw before that a man in his own* πρόσωπον *made use of the* πρόσωπον *of God*[1]. The prophets, it is true, were to a certain extent the representatives of God[2], for *delegates are substitutes of the persons of those who sent them and because of this they are their* πρόσωπα *by virtue of their ministry*[3]. But in Christ the man in the real sense used the πρόσωπον of God, for *Christ has said:* "*My father and I are one*," *and:* "*He who has seen me, has seen the father*[4]," and all honour due to the *Logos* is partaken of by the manhood, because it has become the πρόσωπον of the *Logos*[5]. Likewise, however, as the *Logos* did not become man by nature, so also the manhood in Christ is not deified by nature. *He who had a beginning, grew and was made perfect,* so Nestorius often declares with Gregory of Nazianzen, *is not God by nature, although he is called so on account of the manifestation which took place gradually*[6]. *He is*

[1] B. 76 = N. 49.   [2] l. c.; comp. B. 82 = N. 53.
[3] B. 83 = N. 54.   [4] B. 76 = N. 49.
[5] B. 348 = N. 223: *Dieu était aussi en lui ce qu'il était lui-même; de sorte que ce que Dieu était en lui pour la formation de son être à son image, lui aussi l'était en Dieu: le prosôpon de Dieu;* B. 350 = N. 224: *L'homme...est Dieu par ce qui est uni.*

[6] Gregory, *ep.* 101, Migne, 37, 18: τὸ γὰρ ἠργμένον ἢ προκόπτον ἢ τελειούμενον οὐ θεός, κἂν διὰ τὴν κατὰ μικρὸν ἀνάδειξιν οὕτω λέγηται; Nestorius, *Liber Herac. e.g.* B. 273 = N. 173; B. 280 = N. 177; B. 283 = N. 179; B. 286 = N. 181; B. 332 = N. 212; B. 349 = N. 224; B. 360 = N. 231.

God by manifestation because he was man by nature[1].
*As regards the manhood he is not divine by nature but
by manifestation*[2].

But this is not all that is to be said; for the
manhood in Christ, according to Nestorius, has really
through the union with the *Logos* become something
which it would not be otherwise. The man in Christ
has the πρόσωπον of the son of God not only in the
sense we have already discussed. For when Nestorius
says that the *union took place in the πρόσωπον of the
son*[3], then this does not mean only that aspect of the
interchange of the πρόσωπα, on account of which the
manhood as really bore the πρόσωπον of the *Logos* as
the latter took up the πρόσωπον of the man[4]. Here a
new idea is to be noticed. *Although*—so Nestorius
says—*the Logos was the son of God even before the
incarnation, nevertheless after having taken on the
manhood, he can no more alone be called the son, lest
we should assert the existence of two sons*[5]. The manhood
has become the son of God *because of the son, united
with it*[6]. Again and again Nestorius repeats that two
sons of God was not his doctrine.

---

[1] B. 349 = N. 224.   [2] B. 288 = N. 182.   [3] B. 231 = N. 140.

[4] Comp. B. 331 = N. 211: *A cause de celui qui l'a pris pour son
prosôpon, celui qui a été pris obtient d'être le prosôpon de celui qui
l'a pris.*

[5] *Nestoriana*, p. 275, 1-5 (condensed).

[6] *Nestoriana*, p. 274, 17: υἱὸς διὰ τὸν συνημμένον υἱόν; *Liber
Heracl.* B. 145 = N. 168: *Cette humanité est dite le Fils de Dieu par
l'union avec le Fils (et non par la nature)*; B. 80 = N. 51:...*et il a*

One will understand this better if a new line of thought is followed, which in Nestorius is clearly shown to us only by the *Treatise of Heraclides.* To Adam the *Logos* as his creator *gave his image in all glory and honour*[1], but Adam lost it for himself and for his descendants[2]. Hence the *Logos* became man *in order to efface the fault of the first man and to give back to his nature the original image*[3]. Only he could do it: *apart from him there was nothing divine or honourable*[4], and only in the manhood could this renovation take place[5]. Nestorius gives in this connection a complete answer to the question: *Cur deus homo*[6]? and it is not

donné à la forme du serviteur (qui est) sa forme, un nom qui l'emporte sur tous les noms, c'est à dire le nom de Fils, auquel tout genou, etc.

[1] B. 90 = N. 58. [2] B. 91 = N. 59; B. 107 f. = N. 70.

[3] B. 91 = N. 59. [4] l.c.

[5] B. 267 = N. 161: *On avait besoin de la divinité adhérente pour... refaire la forme de l'image qui avait été détruite par nous; (on avait besoin) aussi de l'humanité qui fut renouvelée et qui reprit sa forme; l'humanité était nécessaire pour observer l'ordre, qui avait existé.*

[6] *e.g.* B. 297 = N. 188: *Dieu le Verbe s'est incarné pour faire de l'humanité la forme de Dieu en lui, et pour le renouveler en lui dans la nature de l'humanité..., parce que lui seul pouvait rénover celui qui était tombé en premier lieu par la transgression de l'inobservance des préceptes; et il donna sa vie pour lui, pour les observer, parce qu'il ne suffisait pas qu'il se conservât sans péché; sinon, notre chute serait demeurée sans guérison comme le paralytique qui se soigne et qui reste sans marcher, mais pour qui le médecin marche, et qui le porte, mais qui ne lui dit pas: " Lève toi (et) marche, car tu a été guéri pour marcher." C'est pourquoi il a pris une forme de serviteur qui était sans péché dans sa création, au point de recevoir dans les observances des préceptes un nom supérieur à tous les noms, et de fortifier, par les observances et par la vigilance, ce qui était dans la rénovation de sa créature.*

88 THE DOCTRINE

only by physical categories as in Athanasius' *de incar-
natione*[1] that Nestorius argues. The idea is further
not exhausted by the thought that the *Logos* took such
a form of a servant, *as was without sin in its creation*[2].
The main thing is that the Logos in the form of a
servant brought into existence a sinless man[3]; hence
the stress is laid on the moral and religious development
of Jesus.

The man alone, even the second Adam, would not
have been able to remain sinless[4]; but *God was acting in
him, and observed the commandments in his place because
he was in this nature*[5]. Christ had all that belongs to
a true man, but *without being deprived of the union with
God the Logos*[6]. *God's will was his own will*[7]; *he
raised his soul to God conforming his volitions to those of
God, so that he was an image of the archetype of the*

---

[1] Migne, ser. graeca 25, 96–197; comp. A. Harnack, *Lehrbuch
der Dogmengeschichte*, 4th edition, Tübingen, 1909, II, 159–162.

[2] *Liber Heracl.* B. 297 = N. 188 (see p. 87, note 6).

[3] *Nestoriana*, p. 239, 19: δείξας ἐν ἑαυτῷ τὸ τῆς φύσεως πρόσωπον
ἁμαρτίας ἐλεύθερον.

[4] *Liber Heracl.* B. 298 = N. 189.   [5] l.c.

[6] B. 133 = N. 86.

[7] B. 102 = N. 67; compare the preceding sentence: *Parce que donc
il s'est humilié en toute chose d'une façon incompréhensible par une
humiliation sans pareille, il est apparu encore un seul esprit, une
seule volonté, une seule intelligence inséparable et indivisible, comme
dans un seul être.* Comp. also *Nestoriana*, fragments, 197, 198, 201
and 202 (pp. 65 f. and 219 f. and 224) the genuineness of which
perhaps may be defended with more confidence than I showed, in
my *Nestoriana* (p. 65 f.).

image of God[1], viz. the *Logos*. So *he renewed our nature in himself by means of a perfect obedience*[2] till the death, to which he *was condemned for us*[3] and through which he, as being sinless, gained the victory over the devil[4]. By means of this renewal *humanity received the form of the sonship of him who had created it*[5]. And together with and by virtue of the gift of sonship there was given to the manhood also a share in the position of power and dominion of the son of God[6].

Now I come to the question: Did Nestorius really make the unity of the natures in the one person of Christ intelligible? As long as one starts by pointing to the *Logos* on the one side and the man on the other, it is comprehensible that a negative answer should have been given. The Antiochian formulas, which are found in Nestorius, *e.g.* διὰ τὸν φοροῦντα τὸν φορούμενον σέβω, διὰ τὸν κεκρυμμένον προσκυνῶ τὸν φαινόμενον[7] and: ὁμολογῶμεν τὸν ἐν ἀνθρώπῳ θεόν, σέβωμεν τὸν τῇ θείᾳ συναφείᾳ τῷ παντοκράτορι θεῷ συμπροσκυνούμενον ἄνθρωπον[8], seem again and again to force

---

[1] B. 96=N. 62; comp. B. 102=N. 66: *La forme de serviteur l'a servi absolument comme il le voulait.*

[2] B. 342=N. 219.　　　[3] B. 102=N. 66.

[4] Comp. B. 297=N. 188; B. 299=N. 189; *Nestoriana*, p. 344 6 ff.

[5] B. 299=N. 189.

[6] *Nestoriana*, p. 361, 22; comp. above, p. 86 f., note 6.

[7] *Nestoriana*, p. 262, 3 f.　　　[8] l.c. p. 249, 2 ff.

us to such a negative answer.   Besides the one πρόσωπον
of Christ we find the two πρόσωπα[1], one of each nature,

[1] Comp. above, p. 78, and B. 348=N. 223: *les prosôpons de l'union.*
Nestorius was even able to write: *Nous ne disons pas union des
prosôpons, mais des natures* (B. 252=N. 152), and as it is not the
translator who is to be blamed for the contradiction to other statements of Nestorius which is to be seen here (comp. above, p. 82,
note 1), it must be conceded that Nestorius in his terminology was not
quite free from inaccuracy (which is to be observed also in his position
toward the comparison of the union in Christ to the union of body and
soul, comp B. 236=N. 142 and B. 292=N. 185).   Nevertheless there
is no real contradiction in Nestorius' thoughts.   What he is denying
(B. 252=N. 152) is one n a t u r a l prosôpon: *C'est pourquoi l'union
a lieu pour le prosôpon et non pour la nature. Nous ne disons pas
union des prosôpons, mais des natures. Car dans l'union il n'y a
qu'un seul prosôpon, mais dans les natures un autre et un autre, de
sorte que le prosôpon soit reconnu sur l'ensemble* (B. 252=N. 152).
This is clearly to be seen also in other passages, *e.g.* B. 304 f.=N. 193:
Ce n'est pas sans prosôpon et sans hypostase que chacune d'elles (viz.
natures) *est connue dans les diversités des natures. On ne conçoit pas
deux prosôpons des fils, ni encore deux prosôpons des hommes, mais
d'un seul homme, qui est mu de la même manière par l'autre. L'union
des prosôpons a eu lieu en prosôpon et non en essence ni en nature. On
ne doit pas concevoir une essence sans hypostase, comme si l'union avait
eu lieu en une essence et qu'il y eut un p r o s ô p o n d ' u n e s e u l e
e s s e n c e. Mais les natures subsistent dans leurs prosôpons et dans
leurs natures et dans le prosôpon d'union. Quant au prosôpon naturel
de l'une, l'autre se sert du même en vertu de l'union; a i n s i il n'y
a qu'un prosôpon pour les deux natures.*—B. 239 = N. 144:...*le prosôpon
de l'une est aussi celui de l'autre et réciproquement.*—B. 333 f. =
N. 212 f.: *La divinité se sert du prosôpon de l'humanité et l'humanité
de celui de la divinité; d e c e t t e m a n i è r e nous disons un seul prosôpon pour les deux.*—B. 340=N. 218: *Ne comprends tu pas, comment
les pères confessent un prosôpon de deux natures? et que les différences
des natures ne sont pas supprimées à cause de l'union parce qu'elles
se réunissent en un seul prosôpon, qui appartient aux natures et a u x
p r o s ô p o n s.*—We need however, a more exhaustive examination of

asserted. There is, as Nestorius himself says, a
difference between *the Lord Jesus Christ* and the
Logos[1]; or: *the terms God-Logos and Christ do not
have the same meaning*[2]. For, *though Christ is not out-
side the Logos*[3], nevertheless the *Logos is not limited
by the body*[4]. Christ spoke of the *Logos as of his*
πρόσωπον *and as if he were one and had the same*
πρόσωπον[5]; *there appeared one spirit, one will, one
inseparable and indivisible intellect as in one being*[6];
*we regard this one as that one and that one as this one,
although this one and that one remain*[7]. But if one
keeps in mind that Nestorius rejected the idea of a
substantial union which would include an alteration
of the *Logos*, then one must say that he came as near
as possible to the idea of a union. Where a substantial
union is excluded, there the union can only come about
on a spiritual plane. Hence Nestorius says that the
incarnation took place *through an intelligent and rational
soul*[8]. By means of the soul a relation is set up between

Nestorius' terminology, especially of the meaning of πρόσωπον in
his works. In B. 240 f.=N. 145 (*Ces choses [corps et âme] s'unis-
sent en une nature et en prosôpon naturel. Dieu prit pour lui
la forme du serviteur et non d'un autre pour son prosôpon et sa
filiation; ainsi sont ceux qui sont unis en une nature. Il
prit la forme du serviteur*, etc.) the words *ainsi sont ceux qui sont
unis en une nature* must have been inadvertently transposed: their
place, in my opinion, is before *Dieu prit pour lui*, etc.

[1] B. 120=N. 133. [2] B. 254=N. 153.
[3] l.c. [4] B. 239=N. 144. [5] B. 79=N. 51.
[6] B. 102=N. 67 (see above, p. 88, note 7: *comme*).
[7] B. 348=N. 223. [8] B. 128=N. 83.

the *Logos* and the man, and this relation is on both
sides one of free will[1], a relation of love[2], a relation
of giving on the one side and of taking on the other[3],
a relation that becomes so close, that the one presents
himself as the other, and that the *form of God* shows
itself in the *form of a servant* and the *form of a servant*
is teaching, acting, etc. in the *form of God.*

We must observe, it is true, that the man is God
not by nature, but only because God reveals Himself in
him, and that the *Logos* is not flesh by nature, but only
manifests himself in the flesh[4]. But also my late
colleague Dr Martin Kähler († Sept. 7th, 1912), who
was regarded as orthodox, held it to be *a vain attempt to
combine two independent beings or two persons in an
individual life*[5]. He himself thought that the union
of the Godhead and manhood will become intelligible
if understood as a reciprocity of two personal actions,

---

[1] B. 264 f. = N. 159 : ...*une union volontaire en prosôpon et non en
nature.*

[2] B. 81 = N. 52 : *unies par l'amour et dans le même prosôpon;*
B. 275 = N. 174 : *réunies en égalité par adhésion (συνάφεια) et par
amour.*

[3] B. 299 = N. 189 f. : ...*afin que le prosôpon fût commun à celui
qui donnait la forme et à celui qui la recevait à cause de son obéissance;*
B. 348 = N. 223 : *Par les prosôpons de l'union l'un est dans l'autre
et cet ' un ' n'est pas conçu par diminution, ni par suppression, ni par
confusion, mais par l'action de recevoir et de donner et par
l'usage de l'union de l'un avec l'autre, les prosôpons recevant et
donnant l'un et l'autre.* [4] Comp. above, p. 83 f. and 85.

[5] Kähler, *Die Wissenschaft der christlichen Lehre*, 3rd edition,
Leipsic, 1905, § 388, p. 339.

*viz. a creative action on the part of the eternal Godhead
and a receiving action on the part of the developing
manhood*[1]. If thus justice is done to the idea of the
unity of the natures in one person, then Nestorius, too,
made it intelligible, even where he, dealing with the
Logos on the one side and the man on the other, tries to
understand the union as the result of the incarnation.
His understanding of πρόσωπον, it is true, does not
coincide with what we mean by "person"—we cannot free
ourselves from metaphysics—but we, too, can sympathise
with him when he took the incarnation as meaning
this, that in the person of Jesus the *Logos* revealed
himself in human form so that the *Logos* exhibited
himself as man and that the man of history was the
manifestation of the *Logos* in such a way that he
exhibited himself to us as the eternal *Logos*[2]. We, too,
therefore, understand what Nestorius means when he
said that the πρόσωπον of the one is also that of the
other.

Still more intelligible does the christology of
Nestorius become to us, if, following his advice, we
start from the one πρόσωπον of the union, *i.e.* from the
one Jesus Christ of history[3]. As regards him we are

[1] l.c.

[2] Comp. *Liber Heracl.* B. 362=N. 233: *l'incarnation est conçue
comme l'usage mutuel des deux (prosôpons) par prise et don.*

[3] *Liber Heracl.* B. 230=N. 139 and in many other places the
prosôpon of the union evidently is the *prosôpon of the flesh.* Comp.
B. 304 f.=N. 193 (above p. 90, note 1): *On ne conçoit pas deux*

able to speak of one person in our sense of the word also. This one person, it is true, is not simply the *Logos*, as this is not limited by the body, but still less is he a mere man. This Jesus Christ of history is the beginner of a new humanity and at the same time the personal revelation of God, and he is the one because he is the other. Only the renewed manhood could become the image of God, but even this was only possible because the God-*Logos* was acting here in the manhood by means of a union of giving and taking[1].

Is this orthodox? The answer I will give in the next lecture.

IV

It was not the personal character of Nestorius which caused his tragic fortune; if he was guilty, it was his doctrine which was to be blamed—this we saw in the preceding lecture. We have tried, therefore, to gain an idea of his teaching. Was Nestorius orthodox? What is his position in the history of dogma?—these are the questions which will occupy us to-day.

The question as to whether Nestorius was orthodox cannot be regarded as really answered by the anathema of the so-called *third ecumenical council of Ephesus*,

prosôpons des fils, ni encore deux prosôpons des hommes, mais d'un seul homme, qui, etc.

[1] Comp. above, p. 88.

because, as we saw[1], an ecumenical council of Ephesus never existed. It was only the party council of Cyril which condemned Nestorius, while the council of the Antiochians was on his side, and the question of doctrine was still undecided even when the council consisting of these two party councils was dissolved. The idea that Nestorius was condemned by "the holy ecumenical council" was only the result of the ecclesiastical-political transactions of which the union of 433 was the outcome[2]. This fiction and the consent of the Antiochians, which they were ignominiously forced to give, cannot help us to decide the question, all the more so since Nestorius could have accepted the doctrinal basis of the peace, although his condemnation was its result.

The standard of measure for Nestorius' doctrine must, therefore, be the definition of that ecumenical council which gave the first decision about the christological question (although proved later to be a preliminary one), viz. the fourth ecumenical council of Chalcedon, of 451.

The definition of this council, which is to be seen not only in its creed but also in its recognition of Leo's letter to Flavian and Cyril's *epistola dogmatica*[3] and *epistola ad Orientales*[4], was a compromise, as the Roman legates could not and would not give up the letter of Leo, while the majority of the Eastern bishops were for

[1] Above, p. 53.   [2] Comp. above, p. 56.
[3] Comp. above, p. 37.   [4] Comp. above, p. 53.

their part tied to the Cyrillian tradition. Without doubt, however, there is no real harmony between these different standards of faith. For Leo's letter declares: *Agit utraque forma cum alterius communione, quod proprium est, verbo scilicet operante quod verbi est et carne exequente quod carnis est; unum horum coruscat miraculis, alterum succumbit injuriis*[1], but Severus of Antioch, the well-known later monophysite, was right, when he said: οὐ γὰρ ἐνεργεῖ ποτε φύσις οὐχ ὑφεστῶσα προσωπικῶς[2], and for Cyril the human nature of Christ was a φύσις οὐχ ὑφεστῶσα, as is shown by his understanding of the ἕνωσις καθ' ὑπόστασιν[3]. Nay, in his *epistola synodica* to Nestorius[4] he even anathematised the διαιρεῖν τὰς ὑποστάσεις μετὰ τὴν ἕνωσιν and required a union of the natures καθ' ἕνωσιν φυσικήν[5]. This disharmony between the Cyrillian tradition and that of the western church represented by Leo showed itself also during the proceedings of the council in a very distinct manner, when the wording of the creed was deliberated. The first draft of this creed contained the words ἐκ δύο φύσεων εἶς[6], which corresponded to the

[1] Ch. iv; Mansi, v, 1375 CD; Hahn, *Bibliothek der Symbole*, 3rd edition, p. 325.

[2] *Doctrina patrum*, ed. F. Diekamp, Münster, 1907, p. 310, 19 f.

[3] Comp. above, p. 72.   [4] Comp. above, p. 44.

[5] *Anath.* 3, Migne, 77, 120 c.

[6] This document was not inserted in the Proceedings (Mansi, VII, 100 D: ὅρον, ὃν ἔδοξε μὴ ἐνταγῆναι τοῖσδε τοῖς ὑπομνήμασι) and now, therefore, is lost, but there cannot be any doubt, that it contained the words ἐκ δύο φύσεων εἶς (comp. Mansi, VII, 103 D:

Cyrillian tradition, but Leo asserted in his letter, that
the unity of Christ's person was seen " in two natures[1],"
and especially blamed Eutyches for not having been
willing to concede the duality of the natures after the
incarnation, while allowing the term ἐκ δύο φύσεων εἷς[2].
The Roman legates, therefore, energetically opposed
the phrase ἐκ δύο φύσεων in the draft of the creed[3]
and they succeeded in substituting ἐν δύο φύσεσιν for
ἐκ δύο φύσεων[4]. One self-consistent view, therefore,
could not be attained in Chalcedon; a compromise
had to be made. And it was made by recognising as
standards of faith at the same time Leo's letter and
Cyril's *epistola dogmatica* and *epistola ad Orientales*[5].
Cyril's *epistola synodica*, which understood the ἕνωσις
καθ᾽ ὑπόστασιν in the sense of a ἕνωσις φυσική, was not

---

definitio...ex duabus naturis habet, and 106 c: *Dioscorus dicebat:*
" *Quod ex duabus naturis est, suscipio, duas non suscipio*"; *sanctis-
simus autem archiepiscopus Leo duas naturas dicit esse in Christo...
Quem igitur sequimini? sanctissimum Leonem, aut Dioscorum?*

[1] Ch. 5, Mansi, v, 1379 b: *Propter hanc unitatem personae in
utraque natura intelligendam* (comp. the preceding note).

[2] Ch. 6, Mansi, v, 1386 f.

[3] Mansi, vii, 101 A B; comp. above, p. 96 f. note 6.

[4] Hahn, *Bibliothek der Symbole*, 3rd edition, p. 166; Hefele,
Conciliengeschichte, 2nd edition, II, 470 f. note 1.

[5] Mansi, vii, 113 B C. The meaning of the sentence τὰς τοῦ
μακαρίου Κυρίλλου...συνοδικὰς ἐπιστολὰς πρός τε Νεστόριον καὶ πρὸς τοὺς
τῆς ἀνατολῆς...ἐδέξατο is illustrated by the fact, that Cyril's *epistola
dogmatica* and *epistola ad Orientales*, but not his *epistola synodica*,
were previously (Mansi, vi, 959 A B, 959 D, 971 A B, 973 c) approved.
Comp. p. 98 note 1.

approved by the council[1], and its creed, by treating the words ὑπόστασις and *persona* as identical, interpreted the term ἕνωσις καθ᾽ ὑπόστασιν in the sense of a *personal* union. By this interpretation Cyril's *epistola dogmatica*, which contained this term[2], was made acceptable to western thought. But even Cyril's *epistola synodica* with its anathematisms, once so sharply attacked by the Antiochians, although it was not recognised, was spared criticism[3]. And more, Dioscorus, Cyril's successor, who had been a more incautious upholder of the Alexandrian tradition than Cyril and who at the Robber-synod had declared the assertion of two natures after the union to be unlawful[4], although he was deposed, was nevertheless not declared a heretic[5]. On the other side also Theodoret, whom a decree of the Robber-synod had deposed[6], was present in Chalcedon. Pope Leo

[1] This is expressly said in the *Collatio cum Severianis* (Mansi, VIII, 821 E—822 A) and is to be seen also in the proceedings of the Chalcedonian council itself (comp. Ermoni, *De Leontio Byzantino*, Paris, 1895, p. 100 f. and 111 f.). I now give up my former opinion, that Cyril's *epistola synodica* was implicitly acknowledged (*Leontius von Byzanz* 1887, p. 50, Hauck's *Real-Encyklopädie*, v, 646, 40).

[2] Migne, 77, 48 B: ἐὰν δὲ τὴν καθ᾽ ὑπόστασιν ἕνωσιν...παραιτούμεθα, ἐμπίπτομεν εἰς τὸ δύο λέγειν υἱούς.

[3] That is less than "acknowledged *implicite*" (comp. above note 1).

[4] Mansi, VI, 737 C.

[5] Mansi, VI, 1094 f., comp. Mansi, VII, 103 B: *Anatolius...dixit: propter fidem non est damnatus Dioscorus, sed quia excommunicationem fecit domino archiepiscopo Leoni et tertio vocatus est et non venit.*

[6] *The second synod of Ephesus together with etc.* ed. by S. G. F. Perry, 1881, pp. 251-258.

had recognised him as orthodox[1], the imperial commissioners stood up for his right to be a member of the council[2], and the synod rehabilitated him after he had consented to anathematize Nestorius[3]. Nevertheless he was not forced to retract his book against Cyril's anathematisms. In the same way Ibas of Edessa, who had likewise been deposed in 449[4], was at Chalcedon reinstated as bishop[5], without having been forced to recant what he had said in his letter to Maris about Cyril's "Apollinarism" as he called it, although this letter had been condemned by the Robber-synod.

Hence it follows, that the decision of Chalcedon was interpreted in very different ways by the western church, by the adherents of Cyril and by Theodoret, Ibas and other Antiochians. It is, therefore, impossible to answer in one sentence the question whether Nestorius was orthodox according to the standard of the Chalcedonian definition.

It is certain that he could have accepted the creed of Chalcedon and its standards of faith as easily as Theodoret, for he could have reconciled himself to Cyril's *epistola dogmatica* if understanding the ἔνωσις καθ' ὑπόστασιν in the sense of a *personal* union, and what Theodoret, yielding to pressure, had anathematized in

[1] Mansi, VII, 190 D.
[2] Mansi, VI, 592 D and VII, 190 B C.
[3] Mansi, VII, 190 A B and 191 B-D.
[4] Perry, l. c. p. 134 f.
[5] Mansi, VII, 262-70.

his old friend[1], Nestorius had never taught, nay he had
even expressly rejected such assertions[2]. Nestorius can
therefore be regarded as orthodox according to the
Antiochian interpretation of the Chalcedonian definition.

The formulas contained in Leo's letter, as we shall
see later more accurately, had their root in a view
somewhat different from that of Nestorius, but Nestorius
had endeavoured more earnestly than Leo to make intelligible the oneness of the person of Christ[3], and in
any case he himself approved of Leo's letter[4]. Thus
according also to the western interpretation of the
Chalcedonian definition Nestorius can be regarded as
orthodox.

On the other hand, an interpretation according to
the Cyrillian tradition could not have been accepted by
Nestorius, and measured by the standard of such an
interpretation he could not be regarded as orthodox.
Such an interpretation, however, had considerable
difficulties. For, while to western thinking Cyril's
letters, which were recognised at Chalcedon, had been
made acceptable by interpretation, there was at that
time in the East no Cyrillian theology, i.e. no theology

[1] Mansi, VII, 189 B: ἀνάθεμα Νεστορίῳ καὶ τῷ μὴ λέγοντι τὴν
ἁγίαν Μαρίαν θεοτόκον καὶ τῷ εἰς δύο υἱοὺς μερίζοντι τὸν ἕνα υἱὸν τὸν
μονογενῆ.

[2] Comp. above p. 31 f. and 74 and his *epistola ad Constantinopolitanos* (comp. above p. 24 f.), ch. 2, Nau, p. 374.

[3] Leo asserted the *unitas personae*, but made no attempt to show
how this *unitas personae* was to be imagined (comp. below p. 113).

[4] See above p. 22.

following the Cyrillian tradition, which could digest
Leo's letter.   The quarrels about the decision of Chalcedon show how disagreeable it was to the majority of
the Eastern Christians.

Hence as long as we apply no other standard than
the Chalcedonian definition, the statement of Professor
Bethune-Baker, that Nestorius was orthodox, is not
to be held a false one.   It was a tragic feature in the
fortune of Nestorius, that he had already been condemned, when the council, whose creed he could have
accepted, was held.

The Chalcedonian definition, however, was not
the final one.   The uncertainty as to how its formulas
were to be interpreted was removed.   The first step of
importance in this direction was the Henotikon of the
Emperor Zeno in 482[1].   This edict, indeed, did not
condemn the Chalcedonian definition, but in actual
opposition to Leo's letter and to its assertion about
the operation of each nature in Christ[2] it expressly
declared: ἑνὸς εἶναί φαμεν τά τε θαύματα καὶ τὰ πάθη[3],
condemning at the same time everyone who then or
earlier, at Chalcedon or elsewhere, thought otherwise[4].
That means that an interpretation of the Chalcedonian
definition according to the Cyrillian tradition only was
to be regarded as right, while Leo's letter with all its

[1] Evagrius, h. e. 3, 14, ed. J. Bidez and L. Parmentier p. 111–114.
[2] See above p. 96.   [3] Evagrius l. c. p. 113, 9.
[4] l. c. p. 113, 21 ff.

contents, which did not suit the Cyrillian point of view, was practically put aside. The eastern church, while under the Henotikon, on the whole enjoyed peace— the Antiochian tradition having been put into the background—, but between it and the western church a schism arose. When in 519 a settlement was reached, the Henotikon being at the same time abrogated, the question as to how the decree of Chalcedon, then reacknowledged, was to be interpreted, came again to the fore in the East.

This time it did not remain long without an answer, for at the same time the activity of the so-called Scythian monks began, and this was important just because they developed a theology wholly along the lines of Cyril, which nevertheless could do justice to all requirements of the Chalcedonian definition[1]. It was scholastic arguing, creation of terms and logical distinctions, which brought into existence this Cyrillian-Chalcedonian orthodoxy. Only one of these saving terms need be mentioned, namely ἐνυποστασία. This term allowed the assertion that the human nature of Christ, although it had no ὑπόστασις of its own, nevertheless was not without ὑπόστασις, the ὑπόστασις of the *Logos* becoming that of the human nature, too. By the help of this term the twofold operation of the natures, spoken of in Leo's letter, could be accepted,

---

[1] Comp. my *Dogmengeschichte*, 4th edition, 1906, p. 304 f. and my *Leontius von Byzanz*, 1887, pp. 60–74.

the one ὑπόστασις of the *Logos* being thought of as
the actual subject of the operation of the divine and
human nature of Christ. Really, however, this doctrine
of the Enhypostasia is identical with the Cyrillian view
of the Anhypostasia of Christ's human nature, for actually
it assumed that the *Logos* and the human nature became
one being in the same sense as understood by Cyril,
when he used the term ἕνωσις φυσική and the phrase
μία φύσις τοῦ θεοῦ λόγου σεσαρκωμένη which had come
in the orthodox tradition through the Apollinaristic
forgeries[1]. There was now only the possibility of
abstract separation of the natures in Christ[2]. As a
shibboleth of their Cyrillian-Chalcedonian orthodoxy,
the Scythian monks used the phrase: ἕνα τῆς ἁγίας
τριάδος πέπονθε σαρκί, and this phrase was really
characteristic. For, like Cyril, it makes the *Logos* the
subject even of the sufferings, while by the addition
of σαρκί, which naturally was not uncyrillian, it was
asserted, that the natures were not mixed through the
union; and to some extent justice was done also to Leo's
letter, which contended that it was the human nature
which suffered. The Antiochian tradition naturally was
considered to be insupportable by this new orthodoxy.
The Scythian monks, therefore, acted consistently in
demanding that Diodore of Tarsus and Theodore of
Mopsuestia, the famous teachers of the Antiochian

[1] Comp. my *Dogmengeschichte*, 4th edition, p. 270 and 293.
[2] Comp. my *Leontius*, p. 71.

school, although they had died in the peace of the
church should be anathematised, as well as Nestorius[1].

This Cyrillian-Chalcedonian orthodoxy was supported
by the emperor Justinian, and the fifth ecumenical
council, held in Constantinople in 553, approved the
emperor's church-policy and the doctrine which he
had supported[2].

The condemnation of Theodore of Mopsuestia and
of the anti-cyrillian writings of Theodoret and Ibas,
sanctioned by this council[3], clearly manifested the fact
that an Antiochian interpretation of the Chalcedonian
definition no longer was allowed. And twice in the
decision of the council an Antiochian interpretation of
Chalcedonian formulas was expressly anathematised[4].
Cyril, therefore, remained master of the field. Even

---

[1] Leontius, *contra Nestorianos et Eutychianos*, 3, 7 ff. and 3, 37 ff.
Migne, *ser. graeca*, 86, 1364–1387.

[2] Comp. the anathematisms of this council, Mansi, IX, 375–388,
Hahn, *Bibliothek der Symbole*, 3rd edition, pp. 168–172.

[3] Anath. 12–14.

[4] Anath. 5: Εἴ τις τὴν μίαν ὑπόστασιν τοῦ κυρίου ἡμῶν Ἰησοῦ
Χριστοῦ οὕτως ἐκλαμβάνει, ὡς ἐπιδεχομένην πολλῶν ὑποστάσεων σημασίαν
καὶ διὰ τούτου...ἐν πρόσωπον λέγει κατὰ ἀξίαν καὶ τιμὴν καὶ προσκύνησιν
καθάπερ Θεόδωρος καὶ Νεστόριος μαινόμενοι συνεγράψαντο· καὶ συκοφαντεῖ τὴν ἁγίαν ἐν Χαλκηδόνι σύνοδον, ὡς κατὰ ταύτην τὴν
ἀσεβῆ ἔννοιαν χρησαμένην τῷ τῆς μιᾶς ὑποστάσεως ῥήματι...ὁ
τοιοῦτος ἀνάθεμα ἔστω.—Anath. 6: Εἴ τις καταχρηστικῶς, ἀλλ' οὐκ
ἀληθῶς, θεοτόκον λέγει τὴν ἁγίαν ἔνδοξον ἀειπαρθένον Μαρίαν ἢ κατὰ
ἀναφοράν, ὡς..., καὶ συκοφαντεῖ τὴν ἁγίαν ἐν Χαλκηδόνι σύνοδον,
ὡς κατὰ ταύτην τὴν ἀσεβῆ ἐπινοηθεῖσαν παρὰ Θεοδώρου ἔννοιαν
θεοτόκον τὴν παρθένον εἰποῦσαν...ὁ τοιοῦτος ἀνάθεμα ἔστω.

his *epistola synodica* actually was approved, for Theodoret and Ibas were criticized for having attacked it[1].

The term ἕνωσις φυσική, used in Cyril's *epistola synodica*, was left, it is true, unapproved; for this term could have been understood as allowing the assumption that the natures in Christ were mixed through their union. Nevertheless, what Cyril really meant by the term ἕνωσις φυσική was accepted; for the ἕνωσις καθ' ὑπόστασιν is interpreted in the sense of an ἕνωσις κατὰ σύνθεσιν[2]. The *Logos* took on—this is the doctrine of the council—a human σάρξ with ψυχή and νοῦς in such a way, that out of the two natures came one Christ[3], who was the subject as of the θαυματουργεῖν so of the παθεῖν[4]; the two natures, of which the one Christ is composed, are only to be distinguished abstractly[5], the *Logos* himself was born a second time through Mary[6], the ἐσταυρωμένος is εἶς τῆς ἀγίας τριάδος[7].

There can · be no doubt, that, measured by the

---

[1] Anath. 13 : Εἴ τις ἀντιποιεῖται τῶν ἀσεβῶν συγγραμμάτων Θεοδωρίτου τῶν κατὰ...τοῦ ἐν ἁγίοις Κυρίλλου καὶ τῶν ιβ' αὐτοῦ κεφαλαίων...καὶ...οὐκ ἀναθεματίζει...πάντας τοὺς γράψαντας κατὰ...τοῦ ἐν ἁγίοις Κυρίλλου καὶ τῶν δώδεκα αὐτοῦ κεφαλαίων...ὁ τοιοῦτος ἀνάθεμα ἔστω. Anath. 14 (against Ibas) has an analogous wording.

[2] Anath. 4 : Ἡ...ἐκκλησία...τὴν ἕνωσιν τοῦ θεοῦ λόγου πρὸς τὴν σάρκα κατὰ σύνθεσιν ὁμολογεῖ, ὅπερ ἐστὶ καθ' ὑπόστασιν.

[3] Anath. 8.   [4] Anath. 3.

[5] Anath. 8.:...τῇ θεωρίᾳ μόνῃ τὴν διαφορὰν', τούτων λαμβάνειν, ἐξ ὧν συνετέθη.

[6] Anath. 2.   [7] Anath. 10 ; comp. 5.

standard of these decisions, the christology of Nestorius is to be called heterodox. It was the main purpose of all the anathematisms of the council to show the Nestorian understanding of the ἕνωσις, of the ἐν πρόσωπον, and of the θεοτόκος, to be heretical.

And these decisions remained valid. The sixth ecumenical council, it is true, in opposition to the Greeks, who were drawing back gradually and too openly from the formulas of Chalcedon, sanctioned the Dyotheletism, asserting, under the strong influence of the western church, the difference between the natures of Christ also as regards the ἐνέργειαι and the φυσικὰ θελήματα[1], but it left the Cyrillian interpretation of the Chalcedonian creed untouched and even gave to the dyotheletic statement a look suited to the Cyrillian tradition; for it said that the human will became in the same sense the real will of the *Logos* as the human flesh became his flesh, the human soul his soul, the human intellect his intellect[2], and that the *Logos* had his being also in the human ἐνεργεῖν and θέλειν[3]. Even if some other parts were added to the apparatus of flesh, soul, intellect, energy, will, which was regarded as composing the human nature, it would not have mattered, since the Cyrillian doctrine had won the

[1] Comp. the creed of the council (approved the 16th of September 861), Mansi, xi, 631–640, the main section of which is to be found also in Hahn, *Bibliothek der Symbole* etc., 3rd edition, pp. 172–174.

[2] Mansi, xi, 637 c d.

[3] l. c. xi, 637 e sq.

victory, and since there existed now in the East a theology which was able to master difficult formulas by means of scholastic distinctions and arguments.

Also the Occident, as far as it belonged to the East-Roman Empire, Rome included, had had to accept the Cyrillian-Chalcedonian orthodoxy of the council of 553; and Rome led the young nations of the mediaeval world in the same direction. When in the Adoptianism of Spain old western tradition, not consistent with the Cyrillian-Chalcedonian orthodoxy, emerged once again, the Carolingian theologians with the agreement of Rome rejected them, and Alcuin in conformity with the Cyrillian-Chalcedonian orthodoxy contended: *in assumptione carnis a deo persona perit hominis, non natura*[1].

There cannot, therefore, be the least doubt, that Nestorius was an exponent of a doctrine which even if not through the decree of Chalcedon, at least through the decisions of later time, was condemned by the church. Hence, measured by the standard of church-orthodoxy, Nestorius—in spite of all Professor Bethune-Baker's attempts to save him—must be regarded as a heretic.

Nevertheless his doctrine has more historical right than the Cyrillian orthodoxy. That is what remains for me to show.

Nestorius was a pupil of the Antiochian school; all

[1] *adv. Felicem* 2, 12, Migne, *ser. latina* 101, 156 A.

Antiochian theologians were at first on his side. He
seems to have endeavoured more earnestly than the
greatest teachers of his school, Diodore of Tarsus and
Theodore of Mopsuestia, to make intelligible the oneness
of the person of Christ. An absolute decision is not
possible in this case, as the chief dogmatic works of
Diodore and Theodore are lost. But even if appearance
speak the truth—I shall return to this question later[1]—it
is nevertheless without doubt, that the fundamental ideas
and the decisive formulas which we find in Nestorius
were part of the traditional teaching of his school.

It was not Diodore or even Theodore who first created
these formulas; they had already been used by Eustathius
bishop of Antioch (who was deposed in 330). We are
able to observe this, although only small fragments of
his works are preserved[2]. It is proved not only by
the idea, that it was not the *Logos* who was born,
who suffered, but the man, whom he joined with

[1] See below p. 126.

[2] The only book of Eustathius which is preserved intact (*De
Engastrimytho*, Migne, *ser. graeca* 18, 613–676) is of little value
here. The fragments of other works were first collected by J. A.
Fabricius (*Bibliotheca graeca* ed. Harles ix, 1804, pp. 136–149)—
these fragments (about 35 in number) are the most important ones—;
in Migne (18, 676–696) the number of fragments is enlarged to
about 50; and a collection of 86 fragments (of which those, which
were formerly known, for the most part are not given in full text) is to
be found in *S. Eustathii, episcopi Antiocheni, in Lazarum, Mariam
et Martham homilia christologica* (which is spurious)...*edita cum
commentario de fragmentis eustathianis opera et studio* Ferdinandi
Cavallera, Paris, 1905.

him¹, whom he resuscitated from the dead², and who then became his σύνθρονος³, and also not only by phrases as ὁ ἄνθρωπος, ὃν ἐφόρησεν⁴, or ἀνθρώπινον ὄργανον⁵ or κατοικοῦσα ἐν αὐτῷ (viz. τῷ ἀνθρώπῳ) θεότης⁶ or ἄνθρωπος θεοφόρος⁷ or ναὸς τῆς θεότητος⁸, but we find

---

¹ *De engastrim.* 17, p. 652 A: ὁ λόγος...ἀρετῇ τῆς θεότητος ἁπανταχοῦ πάρεστιν ἀθρόως. εἰ δὲ καί...τὸν ἔκκριτον αὐτοῦ ναὸν ἐπέτρεψε λυθῆναι, τριήμερον μὲν αὐτίκα πάλιν ἀνήγειρε (comp. 18, p. 653: θεότητος ἀρετῇ... πάντα πληροῖ)—; Cavallera, 15, p. 72 = Migne, p. 685 c: οὐδὲ ὁ λόγος αὐτοῦ...ἀλλ' ὁ ἄνθρωπος τοῦ Χριστοῦ ἐκ νεκρῶν ἐγειρόμενος ὑψοῦται—; Migne, p. 681 c (Cav. 30): ἀπαθὲς τὸ θεῖον τοῦ Χριστοῦ πνεῦμα—; Migne, p. 693 (Cav. 73): *Si in Christo plenitudo divinitatis inhabitat, aliud...inhabitatur; si vero naturaliter differunt ab alterutris, neque mortis passionem, neque cibi appetitum...plenitudini divinitatis coexistere fas est..., homini vero haec applicanda sunt proprie, qui ex anima constat et corpore*—; Migne, p. 691 (Cav. 65): *hominem causa salutis hominum Verbo coaptavit* (συνῆψεν)—; Migne, p. 684 A (Cav. 27): τὸ μὲν γὰρ σῶμα...ἐσταυροῦτο, τὸ δὲ θεῖον τῆς σοφίας πνεῦμα καὶ τοῦ σώματος εἴσω διῃτᾶτο καὶ τοῖς οὐρανίοις ἐπεβάτευε καὶ πᾶσαν περιεῖχε τὴν γῆν—; comp. Migne, 681 B (Cav. 29), p. 684 c (Cav. 28), Cav. 55, p. 90 = Migne, p. 689 B, Cav. 83, p. 99 etc.

² Cav. 16, p. 72 = Migne, p. 685 c: τοῦ λόγου τε καὶ θεοῦ τὸν ἑαυτοῦ ναὸν ἀξιοπρεπῶς ἀναστήσαντος—; comp. Cav. 13, p. 71 and Migne, 677 B (Cav. 25): Joh. 2, 19; Migne, p. 681 c (Cav. 30) and the preceding note.

³ Cav. 14, p. 71 f. = Migne, p. 685 B: σύνθρονος ἀποδέδεικται τῷ θειοτάτῳ πνεύματι διὰ τὸν οἰκοῦντα θεὸν ἐν αὐτῷ διηνεκῶς.

⁴ Migne, p. 677 c (Cav. 26), p. 677 c (Cav. 21).

⁵ Migne, p. 680 c (Cav. 20).

⁶ Cav. 12, p. 69 = Migne, 688 B: θεὸς ἐκ θεοῦ γεννηθεὶς ὁ χρίσας, ὁ δὲ χρισθεὶς ἐπίκτητον εἴληφεν ἀρετήν, ἐκκρίτῳ ναουργίᾳ κοσμηθεὶς ἐκ τῆς τοῦ κατοικοῦντος ἐν αὐτῷ θεότητος, comp. note 3.

⁷ Migne, p. 693 (Cav. 77 and 78): *deiferum hominem; homo deum ferens.*

⁸ Migne, p. 677 B (Cav. 25): ναὸς γὰρ κυρίως ὁ καθαρὸς καὶ ἄχραντος ἡ κατὰ τὸν ἄνθρωπόν ἐστι περὶ τὸν λόγον σκηνή, ἔνθα προφανῶς

him also, however sharply he distinguished between
the *Logos* and the man in Christ, asserting the oneness
of the πρόσωπον, the μοναδικὸν πρόσωπον, in contrast
to the oneness of the natures which was taught by the
Arians[1]. He, too, spoke of the *Logos* (or of the pre-
existent son of God) as the image of God, and of Christ
as the image of the son of God or the image of the
archetype of the image of God[2]; he too—only to
mention one further line of thought common to him
and Nestorius—dealt with Melchisedek as a type of
Christ, in order to refute by means of Hebrews vii. 3
(ἀπάτωρ, ἀμήτωρ) the idea, that the *Logos* was born[3].
The theological tradition followed by Nestorius can
thus be traced at least to Eustathius.

But it dates from a still earlier period. To prove
this, I will start by pointing to the fact that Nestorius
himself found in Leo's letter views which agreed with

σκηνώσας ᾤκησεν ὁ θεός—; Migne, p. 684 c (Cav. 28): πάσχει μὲν
ὁ νεώς—; comp. p. 109 notes 1, 2 and 6.

[1] Cavallera, 7, p. 67: μοναδικὸν τὸ πρόσωπον· οὐκ εἶπον μοναδικὴν
τὴν φύσιν..., ἀλλ' εἶπον ἕνα κύριον Ἰησοῦν Χριστὸν...ἐν τῷ διαφόρῳ τῶν
φύσεων γνωριζόμενον—; comp. Cav. 82, p. 98.

[2] Migne, p. 677 c d (Cav. 21): οὐ γὰρ εἶπεν ὁ Παῦλος (Rom.
8, 29) συμμόρφους τοῦ υἱοῦ τοῦ θεοῦ, ἀλλὰ συμμόρφους τῆς εἰκόνος τοῦ
υἱοῦ αὐτοῦ· ἄλλο μέν τι δεικνύων τὸν υἱὸν εἶναι, ἄλλο δὲ τὴν εἰκόνα αὐτοῦ·
ὁ μὲν γὰρ υἱός...εἰκών ἐστι τοῦ πατρός..., ὁ δὲ ἄνθρωπος, ὃν ἐφόρεσεν, εἰκών
ἐστι τοῦ υἱοῦ—; comp. p. 693 (Cav. 70) and Cavallera 45² p. 85: τὸ
γοῦν τῆς ψυχῆς ὄμμα ἀδόλωτον ἔχοντες πρὸς τὸ τῆς ⟨υἱότητος?⟩ πρωτό-
τυπον καὶ τῆς εἰκόνος μόρφωμα προσβλέποντες δοξάζομεν τὸ τῆς εἰκόνος
ἀρχέτυπον, comp. Cav. 82, p. 98, where Baruch 3, 36–38 is quoted.

[3] Cavallera, 3, p. 63.

his own. Leo was not the author of these views; he, too, followed a tradition which had come down to him. A generation before Leo a very striking agreement with Nestorius is seen in Pelagius, a native of Britain[1]. He says about the *Logos, quem ubique esse non dubium est: descenderat ad formam servi non localiter, sed dignanter*[2], and even the following sentence is found in him: *omnes simul hominem adorent cum verbo assumptum*[3]. It is not wholly improbable that these formulas of Pelagius were influenced by the Antiochian theology, for it is possible that Pelagius visited the East before he came to Rome. But even if Pelagius be left out of consideration (although his utterances may be wholly explained as having their origin in western tradition),—even then a near relationship between the western and the Antiochian tradition can easily be proved. As early as in Tertullian's time, one spoke in the West of two natures of Christ which were not mixed but joined (*conjunctae = συνημμέναι*[4]) and Tertullian himself says[5]: *adeo salva est utriusque*

---

[1] Comp. Hauck's *Real-encyklopädie* xxiv, 1913, p. 312, 30 ff.

[2] On Eph. 4, 9, Migne, *ser. lat.* 30, 1846, p. 832 A, comp. Zimmer, *Pelagius in Irland*, p. 365.

[3] On Phil. 2, 10, Migne, p. 846 A, Zimmer, l. c. p. 378. Comp. other striking quotations in my *Leitfaden zum Studium der Dogmengeschichte*, 4th edition, p. 287 f.

[4] Comp. Tertullian *adv. Praxeam* 27: *Videmus duplicem statum, non confusum, sed conjunctum, in una persona, deum et hominem Jesum.*

[5] *adv. Praxeam* l. c.

proprietas substantiae, ut et spiritus (i.e. the *Logos*[1])
*res suas egerit in illo, id est virtutes, et caro passiones
suas functa sit, denique et mortua.*   The phrases " *homo
Christi,*" "*assumptus homo*" or "*susceptus homo*" are very
often found in the west even as late as in Augustine[2].
The idea of the coexistence of the *forma servi* and the
forma dei, which we found in Nestorius, belonged here
to the tradition[3], and in Novatian (about 250) we find
the idea, returning even in the 8th century in the
Adoptianism of Spain, that by the son of God by
nature the son of man also, whom he joined to himself
and who was not son of God by nature, was made
a son of God[4], and as late as in the 4th century
Ambrosius says about the words on the cross: " My
God, my God, why hast thou forsaken me ? " *clamavit
homo divinitatis separatione moriturus*[5].

[1] Comp. about Eustathius above p. 109 notes 1 and 3 and about
other western theologians Loofs, *Das Glaubensbekenntnis der Homousianer v. Sardica (Abhandlungen der Berliner Akademie,* 1909, p. 35).

[2] Comp. Harnack, *Dogmengeschichte,* 4th edition, ɪɪ, 358 ff.;
Loofs, *Dogmengeschichte,* 4th edition, p. 284 ff. Augustine often
used the term *dominicus homo* (comp. O. Scheel, *Die Anschauung
Augustins von Christi Person und Werk,* 1901, p. 228) and only as
late as *Retract* 19, 8 (Migne, *ser. lat.* 32, 616) blamed this expression.

[3] Comp. J. B. Lightfoot's Commentary, 127–135; H. Reuter,
Augustinische Studien, 1887, p. 198 ff.; O. Scheel, l. c. p. 189 ff.;
Leo, *ep. ad Flavianum,* ch. 3.

[4] Novatian *de trin.* 24 (al. 19), Migne, *ser. lat.* 3, 933 c:
legitimus dei filius, qui ex ipso deo est,...dum sanctum istud (comp.
Luke 1, 35) *assumit, sibi filium hominis annectit et...filium illum dei
facit, quod ille naturaliter non fuit.*

[5] *in Luc.* 10, 127, Migne, *ser. lat.* 15, 1836 A.

There was, it is true, a difference between western and Antiochian thinking, for, while all Antiochians, Nestorius included, even when starting with the *Logos* endeavoured to make intelligible the oneness of the person of Christ, that is, to use Melanchthon's[1] words, to explain the *modus incarnationis,* the Westerners did not trouble themselves with this difficulty. The oneness of the person of the Jesus of history—"*persona*" being here more than the πρόσωπον of the Antiochians and nearer to what we understand by "*person*"—was with the western theologians an indisputable fact, which was presupposed in all their christological explanations. About this one person they asserted, that it was the *filius dei incarnatus* and also that two distinct *substances* or *natures* were clearly to be seen in it[2]. The speculative question as to how this was to be conceived did not occupy the western church; the doctrine of two natures meant here nothing more than that only afterwards one discerned in this one person the two natures; and the presupposition of the oneness of the person of him who was God and man together was here regarded without any efforts of thought as so certain, that because of this oneness of the person the phrases *deus natus est* and *crucifixus est* were used in early times[3].

[1] *Loci* of 1521, *Corpus Ref.* 21, 85.

[2] Comp. above p. 111, note 4.

[3] Tertullian, *de carne Christi* 5; Damasus, *epigramma* 91, ed. M. Ihm, p. 94; Reuter, *Augustinische Studien*, p. 205 ff.

The western theologians were, however, aware of the fact, that such phrases were only inaccurate and incomplete statements, for only by virtue of the addition "*ex humana substantia*" did these phrases suit the undivided Christ, while as regards the *Logos* they were nothing more than forms of speech[1].

Nevertheless, in spite of this difference there can, in my opinion, be no doubt, that there must have been a kinship between the western and the Antiochian tradition. Adolf Harnack, it is true, does not admit this. He says that the Antiochians were going the same way as Paul of Samosata[2], and he even thinks that the explanations of Theodore of Mopsuestia about the relation of the *Logos* and the man in Christ, and about Christ's natures, will, feelings and so on were, here and there, literally identical with those of Paul of Samosata[3]. The christology of Paul of Samosata, as to itself, is considered by him to be an advanced form of the christology of Hermas and the so-called Monarchians of Rome[4]. Between Tertullian's doctrine of two natures in Christ, however, and the doctrine of the Monarchians he sees no connection; he looks upon Tertullian's doctrine, in so far as it goes farther than Irenaeus on whose works Tertullian was dependent, as formulated by Tertullian

[1] Tertullian *adv. Praxeam* 29 and Reuter l. c.—Even Leo, *ep. ad Flavianum* 5, says: *filius dei crucifixus dicitur, cum haec non in divinitate ipsa..., sed in naturae humanae sit infirmitate perpessus.*

[2] *Dogmengeschichte* II[1], 324; II[4], 339.

[3] l. c. I[1], 599; I[4], 732.   [4] I[1], 594; I[4], 727.

himself and influenced by Gnostic ideas[1]. Besides in Harnack it is not clear whether these relations are to be regarded as based on mere resemblance or on real kinship, for he remarks even as regards the connection between Eustathius and the later Antiochians, that in consequence of the many crossings it would be very difficult to prove a direct dependence and influence. He thinks it must suffice to group together what is homogeneous[2]. I cannot share this sceptical attitude— in the course of my research into the history of dogma I have become increasingly more convinced of the influence of tradition—, and the very kinships assumed here by my honoured teacher and friend do not seem to me to be the right ones[3]. In my opinion the supposition that there was a kinship in tradition between the Antiochian and the western christology seems to be unavoidable because of the close resemblance of the views and the formulas. But what sort

[1] I[1], 474; I[4], 606.   [2] II[4], 341 note 1.

[3] I do not deny that there was a kinship in tradition between Paul of Samosata, bishop of Antioch, and the later Antiochians. The famous passages of Paul in the *Doctrina patrum* (*ed.* Diekamp, p. 303 IV—304 VIII), about the genuineness of which I am more doubtful than Harnack (*Dogmengeschichte* I[4], 724 note 1), especially the most interesting of them (l. c. p. 304 VIII: τὰ κρατούμενα τῷ λόγῳ τῆς φύσεως κ.τ.λ.), could have been written by Theodore of Mopsuestia or by Nestorius. But Paul of Samosata was not the creator of the formulas he used; he stood in the same line of tradition as Eustathius, Theodore and Nestorius, although he modified these traditions— perhaps, however (comp. Harnack I[4], 724 note 2), not in such a degree, as his opponents try to make us believe.

of kinship was it? To answer this question I must
enlarge upon two other points, *i.e.* the doctrine of
Marcellus of Ancyra and the so-called *Symbolum
Sardicense.*

Marcellus of Ancyra, whose huge work is preserved
only in fragments[1], does not seem to have occupied
himself with the christological question as such, as far
as we can judge. It was the Arian *Logos*-doctrine
that he opposed; the Arian doctrine as to the Jesus
of history was not made an object of discussion by him.
Hence it may be explained, that in some places he says:
the *Logos* took on *flesh,* and in others: God joined a
man to his *Logos.* This latter phrase, it is true, is less
often used than the other, but nevertheless it does occur[2].
And it is not this phrase alone which shows resemblance
to Nestorius' doctrine; it is also said by Marcellus, that
the man joined to the *Logos* became son of God by adop-
tion ($\theta \acute{\epsilon} \sigma \epsilon \iota$)[3], and we even find in him the idea, that this

---

[1] Collected after Rettberg (*Marcelliana*, Göttingen, 1794) by
E. Klostermann (*Eusebius Werke* IV, *Gegen Marcell.*, etc., Leipzig,
1906), pp. 185–215. Comp. F. Loofs, *Die Trinitätslehre Marcells v.
Ancyra* (*Sitzungsberichte der Berliner Akademie*, 1902, pp. 764–781).

[2] Klostermann, 74, p. 200, 5 f.: οὐκ εἰς τὸν ἄνθρωπον ὃν ἀνείληφεν ἀποβλέπων τοῦτό (John 10, 30) φησιν, ἀλλ' εἰς τὸν ἐκ τοῦ πατρὸς
προελθόντα λόγον—; 1, p. 185, 10: ὅτε τὸν ἀγαπηθέντα ὑπ' αὐτοῦ
ἄνθρωπον τῷ ἑαυτοῦ συνῆψεν λόγῳ—; comp. 107, p. 208, 15; 108,
p. 208, 22; 117, p. 210, 29.

[3] Klostermann, 41, p. 192, 1 ff.: καὶ διὰ τοῦτο οὐχ υἱὸν θεοῦ
ἑαυτὸν ὀνομάζει, ἀλλὰ...υἱὸν ἀνθρώπου..., ἵνα διὰ τῆς τοιαύτης ὁμολογίας
θέσει τὸν ἄνθρωπον διὰ τὴν πρὸς αὐτὸν κοινωνίαν υἱὸν θεοῦ γενέσθαι
παρασκευάσῃ.

man joined to the *Logos*[1], after having been exalted, became σύνθρονος τῷ θεῷ[2]. Still more of kinship in tradition is to be seen between Marcellus and Nestorius when in Marcellus Christ appears as the beginner of a new humanity. It was for this purpose, that the *Logos* took on the man, viz. that he might assist the man who has been deprived by the devil of his position of glory, in gaining victory over the latter[3]. He, the man joined to the *Logos*, is the πρωτότοκος τῆς καινῆς κτίσεως and the πρωτότοκος ἐκ νεκρῶν[4], the πρῶτος καινὸς ἄνθρωπος, εἰς ὃν τὰ πάντα ἀνακεφαλαιώσασθαι ἐβουλήθη ὁ θεός[5], he is the image of the *Logos* and thus of the invisible God[6], and, having become κύριος and θεός[7], he received thereby the firstfruits of the

---

[1] Klostermann, 42, p. 192, 8 and 109, p. 208, 25: ὁ τῷ λόγῳ ἐνωθεὶς ἄνθρωπος.   [2] Klostermann, 110, p. 208, 30.

[3] l. c. 108, p. 208, 21 ff.: ἵνα ὑπὸ τοῦ διαβόλου ἀπατηθέντα πρότερον τὸν ἄνθρωπον αὐτὸν αὖθις νικῆσαι τὸν διάβολον παρασκευάσῃ· διὰ τοῦτο ἀνείληφεν τὸν ἄνθρωπον, ἵνα ἀκολούθως τοῦτον ἀπαρχὴν τῆς ἐξουσίας παραλαβεῖν παρασκευάσῃ.

[4] l. c. 2, p. 185, 24: οὐ μόνον τῆς καινῆς κτίσεως πρωτότοκον αὐτὸν ὁ ἀπόστολος εἶναι φησίν, ἀλλὰ καὶ πρωτότοκον ἐκ νεκρῶν.

[5] l. c. 6, p. 186, 18 f.

[6] l. c. 94, p. 205, 12 ff.: εἰκών ἐστιν τοῦ ἀοράτου θεοῦ· νῦν δηλονότι, ὁπηνίκα τὴν κατ᾽ εἰκόνα τοῦ θεοῦ γενομένην ἀνείληφε σάρκα...εἰ γὰρ διὰ τῆς εἰκόνος ταύτης τὸν τοῦ θεοῦ λόγον ἠξιώθημεν γνῶναι, πιστεύειν ὀφείλομεν αὐτῷ τῷ λόγῳ διὰ τῆς εἰκόνος λέγοντι· ἐγὼ καὶ ὁ πατὴρ ἕν ἐσμεν. οὔτε γὰρ τὸν λόγον οὔτε τὸν πατέρα τοῦ λόγου χωρὶς τῆς εἰκόνος ταύτης γνῶναί τινα δυνατόν.

[7] l. c. 111, p. 209, 1 f.: τὸν ἄνθρωπον τὸν πρότερον διὰ τὴν παρακοὴν τῆς βασιλείας ἐκπεπτωκότα κύριον καὶ θεὸν γενέσθαι βουλόμενος ὁ θεὸς ταύτην τὴν οἰκονομίαν εἰργάσατο.

position of power which is given back to man[1]. Finally
it is deserving of notice, that Marcellus, when applying
the terms υἱός, κύριος and Χριστός only to the Christ
of history, is, as regards the two latter terms, in perfect
harmony with Nestorius, and that further, as regards the
first, Nestorius, too, applied the term after the incarnation only to the undivided historical person of Christ[2].
I have, therefore, no doubt that there existed a kinship
in tradition between Marcellus and Nestorius[3]. I do
not mean that Nestorius had necessarily read Marcellus'
work. It is probable—if a conjecture as to the text
is right—that he once named[4] him, opposing his idea,
that the *Logos*, when going at the end of all things to
be reabsorbed into the Father, would put off his flesh;
but he could have learned this idea through hearsay.
Marcellus and Nestorius could have a kinship in

---

[1] See p. 117, note 3, comp. above p. 89 at note 8.

[2] See above p. 86.

[3] In consideration of the fact that a common kinship of two
persons to a third one proves them to be akin to one another, I notice
that we find in Marcellus and E u s t a t h i u s the same understanding
of the ὁμοούσιος as excluding *persons* (ὑποστάσεις) in the Trinity, the
same use of πνεῦμα as applied to the L o g o s, the same quotation of
Baruch, 3, 36–38 (comp. above p. 110, note 2, and Marcellus, fragm.
70, p. 202, 20 ff.) and the same striking explanation of Prov. 8, 22
(comp. Eustathius, fragm. C a v a l l e r a, 33, p. 77: ἀρχὴ γάρ τοι τῶν
καλλίστων τῆς δικαιοσύνης ὁδῶν γεγένηται ἡμῖν ὁ ἄνθρωπος τοῦ Χριστοῦ,
τοῖς κρείττοσι τῶν ἐπιτηδευμάτων προσάγων ἡμᾶς κ.τ.λ. and Marcell,
fragm. 9–15, K l o s t e r m a n n, p. 186 f.).

[4] *Nestoriana*, p. 298, 23, where *Marcellus* is substituted for
Manichaeus.

tradition even if Nestorius did not know Marcellus' work. Besides it is perhaps remarkable, that Nestorius who so zealously anathematises all heretics never put Marcellus on such a black list.

Likewise it seems to me without doubt, that there is a kinship in tradition between Nestorius and the so-called *Symbolum Sardicense*[1]. In the beginning of this creed Ursacius and Valens, "the Arians," as they are called, are blamed because they pretended to be Christians, and nevertheless dared to say, that the "*Logos* or Spirit" was wounded, slain, died and rose again[2]. Correspondingly the creed declares at the end, that not the Spirit in Christ (*i.e.* the *Logos*) suffered, ἀλλ᾿ ὁ ἄνθρωπος, ὃν ἐνεδύσατο, ὃν ἀνέλαβεν ἐκ Μαρίας τῆς παρθένου, τὸν ἄνθρωπον τὸν παθεῖν δυνάμενον[3], and it asserts as to the resurrection that not ὁ θεὸς ἐν τῷ ἀνθρώπῳ ἀλλ᾿ ὁ ἄνθρωπος ἐν τῷ θεῷ ἀνέστη[4]. This conformity of views between the *Sardicense* and Nestorius is really not surprising, for the *Sardicense* is of western origin and we have already seen that since Tertullian's time the western tradition included a doctrine of the two natures of Christ, which resembled that of Nestorius[5].

---

[1] I quote the revised text I gave in *Das Glaubensbekenntnis der Homousianer von Sardica* (*Abhandlungen der Berliner Akademie*, 1909) pp. 7-11.

[2] 3, p. 7, 7-10.   [3] 11, p. 10, 53-55.   [4] *ib.* p. 10, 55 f.

[5] Comp. the references to western theologians I gave in the notes of *Das Glaubensbekenntnis* etc. (p. 11 ff.).

Moreover, as regards the relation between Nestorius
and the *Sardicense* another point, too, is to be discussed.
I must go a roundabout way to show this. First,
attention must be drawn to the fact that the *Sardicense*
had a particular kinship with Marcellus[1]. Like Marcellus, the *Sardicense* declares that the term πρωτότοκος,
if used of Christ, is applied to him as to the new
creature, *i.e.* as to the beginner of the new humanity[2].
Like Marcellus, it understands the eternity of the *Logos*,
not as Origen did as an eternal existence beside God
the Father, but as the eternal existence in him up
to the time when he issued from God[3]. Like Marcellus,
the *Sardicense* contends that God and his *Logos* have
one ὑπόστασις[4]. Like Marcellus, it identifies the λόγος
ἄσαρκος and the Spirit of God[5]; and like Marcellus, it
assumes, that from the historical Christ the Spirit of
God proceeded and went over to the disciples[6]. Like

---

[1] This, too, is proved in the notes mentioned in the preceding
note.

[2] Comp. above p. 117, note 4, and *Sardicense*, 7, p. 9: ὁμολογοῦμεν
μονογενῆ καὶ πρωτότοκον· ἀλλὰ μονογενῆ τὸν λόγον, ὃς πάντοτε ἦν καὶ
ἔστιν ἐν τῷ πατρί· τὸ πρωτότοκος δὲ τῷ ἀνθρώπῳ διαφέρει (*i.e.* refers to
the man) καὶ τῇ καινῇ κτίσει, ὅτι καὶ πρωτότοκος ἐκ νεκρῶν.

[3] Comp. the preceding note.

[4] *Sardicense*, 4, p. 7: ἡμεῖς δὲ ταύτην παρειλήφαμεν...πίστιν καὶ
ὁμολογίαν· μίαν εἶναι ὑπόστασιν,...τοῦ πατρὸς καὶ τοῦ υἱοῦ καὶ τοῦ ἁγίου
πνεύματος.

[5] *Sardicense*, 11, p. 10: καὶ τοῦτο (viz. τὸ πνεῦμα) πιστεύομεν
πεμφθέν· καὶ τοῦτο οὐ πέπονθεν, ἀλλ' ὁ ἄνθρωπος, ὃν ἐνεδύσατο.

[6] This cannot be proved by a single quotation; but evidence is
given in my papers *Die Trinitätslehre Marcells* (p. 771 ff.) and *Das*

Marcellus, therefore, the *Sardicense* teaches an economic-trinitarian monotheism, *i.e.* the Trinity does not appear here as eternal, but as produced in the course of the economy, *i.e.* of God's dispensation. God was according to Marcellus originally an absolute μονάς, then the *Logos* issued from him as his δραστικὴ ἐνέργεια without being separated from him δυνάμει, and then from the *incarnate Logos* the Spirit proceeded, the Spirit of God, who was in him and went over to the Christian community. These views were without doubt shared by the *Sardicense*, although they are not all definitely expressed. It did not even blame another idea of Marcellus which is closely connected with these views, viz. that just as the divine μονάς has been extended, the Spirit and the *Logos* will finally be reabsorbed in God in order that God may be all in all; for this idea, in spite of all opposition to it on the part of Marcellus' enemies, is passed over in silence by the *Sardicense*, and, as I have shown elsewhere[1], this silence was not merely the result of church-policy, *i.e.* it cannot be explained by the fact, that Marcellus, in contradiction to the majority of the eastern bishops but in harmony with the western, held to the Nicene creed. The real reason was, that the idea of Marcellus here in question corresponded to a tradition found in Tertullian and Novatian

Glaubensbekenntnis etc. (p. 31 ff.). Also regarding the statements which follow above I must refer to these papers.

[1] In the papers mentioned note 6, p. 120.

and found in the western church as late as the middle
of the 4th century[1].

Now it is theoretically possible that Marcellus was
influenced by the western tradition existing long before
his time, although it is very improbable that western
tradition could have made such an impression on an
eastern theologian. Actually, however, this is quite

[1] Comp. my paper *Das Glaubensbekenntnis* etc., p. 31–34. Only
four quotations may be given here: Tertullian, *adv. Praxeam*, ch. 4 ed.
Kroymann, p. 232, 16 ff.: *cum autem subjecta erunt illi omnia absque
eo, qui ei subjecit omnia, tunc et ipse subjicietur illi, qui ei subjecit
omnia, ut sit deus omnia in omnibus* (1 Kor. 15, 28). *videmus igitur
non obesse monarchiae* [*filium*], *etsi hodie apud filium est, quia et in suo
statu est apud filium et cum suo statu restituetur patri a filio.*—
Novatian, *de trin.* 3, Migne, *ser. lat.* 3, 952 A: *subjectis enim ei quasi
filio omnibus rebus a patre* etc. (1 Kor. 15, 28), *totam divinitatis
auctoritatem rursus patri remittit; unus deus ostenditur verus et
aeternus pater, a quo solo haec vis divinitatis emissa et jam in filium
tradita et directa rursum per substantiae communionem ad patrem
revolvitur.*—Victorinus Afer († circ. 363), *adv. Arianos*, 1, 39, Migne,
ser. lat. 8, p. 1070 D: *evacuatis enim omnibus, requiescit activa
potentia* (i.e. the *Logos*) *et erit in ipso deo secundum quod est esse
et secundum quod est quiescere, et in aliis autem spiritualiter secundum
suam et potentiam et substantiam, et hoc est "ut sit deus omnia in
omnibus," non enim omnia in unoquoque, sed deo existente in omnibus,
et ideo omnia erit deus, quod omnia erunt deo plena.*—Zeno of Verona
(about 370), after having quoted 1 Kor. 15, 24 ff. on the one side and
Luke 1, 32 (*regni ejus non erit finis*) and Sap. 3, 4 ff. (*regnabit dominus
eorum in perpetuum*) on the other: *quid hoc est? si in perpetuum
regnat, Paulus erravit; si traditurus est regnum, isti mentiuntur.
absit! nullus hic error, diversitas nulla est. Paulus enim de hominis
assumpti temporali locutus est regno..., hi autem ad princi-
palem vim retulerunt, in cujus perpetuitate commanens in aeternum,
a patre filius regnum nec accepit aliquando, nec posuit; semper enim
cum ipso regnavit.*

impossible; for it is admitted by all that the origin of the ideas of Marcellus can be sufficiently explained by an earlier eastern theological tradition. This latter is seen in Irenaeus, a native of Asia Minor, about 185, although it is in him influenced by the quite different views of the apologists[1]. Before Irenaeus it is to be found in the utterances of the presbyters of Asia Minor which are quoted in several places by Irenaeus[2]. Even in the beginning of the second century, about 110, we meet ideas resembling the fundamental thoughts of Marcellus in Ignatius, bishop of Antioch, who, as is shown in the course of his last journey through Asia Minor and by his relation to the Gospel of John, must have had intercourse with Asia Minor before becoming bishop. Like Marcellus, Ignatius assumes that the *Logos* of God is not begotten[3]; like Marcellus and differing from the apologists, he applies the term *Son of God* only to the historical and exalted Christ[4]; like Marcellus he nevertheless speaks about an issuing of the *Logos* from God[5]; like Marcellus, he says that God, when the *Logos* issued from him, broke his silence[6], *i.e.* opened

[1] Comp. my *Dogmengeschichte*, 4th edition, § 21, 2d, p. 143 f.

[2] l. c. § 15, 6, p. 103.

[3] *ad Ephes.* 7, 2: εἷς ἰατρός ἐστιν, σαρκικός τε καὶ πνευματικός, γεννητὸς (as σαρκικός) καὶ ἀγέννητος (as πνευματικός) κ.τ.λ.

[4] Comp. the preceding note and *ad Smyrn.* 1, 1: υἱὸν θεοῦ κατὰ θέλημα καὶ δύναμιν θεοῦ γεγεννημένον...ἐκ παρθένου.

[5] *ad Magn.* 7, 2: Ἰησοῦν Χριστόν, τὸν ἀφ' ἑνὸς πατρὸς προελθόντα.

[6] Marcellus, fragm. 103, Klostermann, p. 207, 25: πρὸ γὰρ τῆς δημιουργίας ἀπάσης ἡσυχία τις ἦν, ὡς εἰκός, ὄντος ἐν τῷ θεῷ τοῦ

the economy, *i.e.* his dispensation which was intended
for the world's salvation; like Marcellus, he speaks
about the οἰκονομία εἰς τὸν καινὸν ἄνθρωπον, *i.e.* about
the dispensation of God which gave in Christ a new
beginning to the humanity[1]; like Marcellus, he probably
identified the λόγος and the Spirit of God as regards
the time before the Spirit went over from the historical
Christ to his disciples[2]. For him as for Marcellus the
historical Christ is at once God revealed in flesh and
the new and perfect man[3]. Finally, it is not improbable that Ignatius, too, supposed that the *Logos* and
the Spirit would at last be reabsorbed in God[4].

Hence dependence of Marcellus on the western
tradition is excluded from possibility. There is also
another argument against it, viz. that even in Tertullian
the western tradition shows itself influenced by the

λόγου—; Ignatius, *ad Smyrn.* 8, 2: Ἰησοῦ Χριστοῦ τοῦ υἱοῦ αὐτοῦ,
ὅς ἐστιν αὐτοῦ λόγος ἀπὸ σιγῆς προελθών.

[1] As regards Marcellus comp. above p. 117, notes 4 and 5, and
Klostermann, Index s.v. οἰκονομία; Ignatius, *ad Ephes.* 20, 1: οἰκο-
νομία εἰς τὸν καινὸν ἄνθρωπον Ἰησοῦν Χριστόν and *ad Smyrn.* 4, 2:
Ἰησοῦ Χριστοῦ...τοῦ τελείου ἀνθρώπου γενομένου.

[2] In Ignatius, *ad Philad. inscriptio*, the πνεῦμα ἅγιον is τὸ ἅγιον
Χριστοῦ πνεῦμα, while, according to *ad Smyrn.* 3, 3, Christ was on
earth πνευματικῶς ἡνωμένος τῷ πατρί; and *ad Rom.* 7, 2, Ignatius
apparently had in mind John 7, 38 f.

[3] Comp. above note 1 and *ad Ephes.* 19, 3: θεοῦ ἀνθρωπίνως
φανερουμένου εἰς καινότητα ἀιδίου ζωῆς.

[4] It seems to me not improbable, that in Ignatius *ad Magnes.*
7, 2 is to be read: ἐπὶ ἕνα Ἰησοῦν Χριστόν, τὸν ἀφ' ἑνὸς πατρὸς προελθόντα
(comp. p. 123, note 5) καὶ εἰς ἕνα ὄντα (comp. John 1, 18) καὶ εἰς ἕνα
χωρήσοντα (instead of χωρήσαντα).

views of the apologists[1], who, to take only one example, applied the term "Son of God" to the pre-existent *Logos* and did not comprehend that the historical Christ was even as the Son of God the beginner of a new humanity[2].

The western tradition, therefore, must be traced back to the very pre-apologetic views which gave birth to the tradition followed by Marcellus. And this connection is at least recognisable for us in one place; for we find that Tertullian was strongly influenced by Irenaeus and Melito, both natives of Asia Minor, and by the Montanistic movement which arose in the same country.

This is the line of tradition in which Nestorius, too, has his place. That has been proved by what I have said about his relation to Eustathius, Marcellus, and the *Sardicense*.

The old tradition shows in him, it is true, in many respects an altered face. Origen had strengthened the influence of the apologists; Nestorius, too, shows many signs of this influence. But the old tradition seems to have

[1] The influence of the apologists on Tertullian needs not to be proved; about the older traditions, which are clearly seen in him, comp. W. Macholz, *Spuren binitarischer Denkweise im Abendlande*, *dissert. theol. Halensis*, 1902, pp. 35–57.

[2] There are in Tertullian remains of the pre-apologetic under-standing of the term "Son of God," e.g. *adv. Praxeam*, 26, *ed.* Kroymann, p. 277, 26: *dicens* (viz. the angel in Luke 1, 35) *autem "Spiritus dei" portionem totius* (viz. *substantiae divinae*) *intelligi voluit, quae cessura erat in filii nomen.*

had more influence on him than on the famous earlier
teachers of his school.   The tendency of his christology
to start from the historical Christ and to apply not
only the terms Χριστός and κύριος but also the term
Son of God only to the historical Lord[1] probably did
not come only from his own endeavour to lay stress on
the oneness of the historical person of Christ, but must
have had a connection with the old tradition which had
come down to him.

If all this is right Nestorius is justified in his
thinking in a higher degree than if he had been
shown to be orthodox in the sense of the later orthodoxy;
for then he is nearer to the oldest theological tradition
and nearer to the N.T. than this later orthodoxy itself.

Only two remarks are to be made in this respect.
We are accustomed to the orthodox trinitarian and
christological formulas as they appear when detached
from the whole to which they originally belonged.
Hence we do not see that in these formulas a mythology,
actually contradicting the monotheistic belief, had
gained the victory.

This is, however, shown just by the contrast between
Nestorius and the Cyrillian orthodoxy.   The council of
553 sanctioned, as we saw[2], the statement of the Scythian
monks τὸν ἐσταυρωμένον σαρκὶ...εἶναι ἕνα τῆς ἁγίας

[1] Comp. *Nestoriana*, *Index*, s.v. Χριστός, κύριος, υἱός and above,
p. 86.
[2] Above p. 105 at note 7.

τριάδος. What weight this sanction had is illustrated
by the remark of the same council, that the Holy
Trinity did not receive any addition when "one of
the Trinity" became man[1]. This remark is purposely
directed against Nestorius, who himself deals with the
reproach, that his doctrine led to the result, that the
man in Christ was added to the Trinity as the fourth
person[2]. He did not give a satisfactory answer to this
reproach[3]. Nor did Marcellus master the difficulty.
For him the problem did not lie in the fact, that on
account of the flesh, he had to regard the historical and
exalted Christ as another beside God, in spite of his
dynamic unity with God, for this is undoubtedly the
view held by the N.T. also; but he confesses, that he
did not know, what would become of the manhood
(*flesh*) of Christ, when the *Logos* should finally be
reabsorbed in the unity of God, so that God might be
all in all[4]. There was no difficulty here for the old
tradition; for when finally all Christians are made
perfect and wholly filled with the Spirit of God, then
naturally the beginner of the new humanity would no
longer have a peculiar position to himself, although

---

[1] Anath. 5: οὔτε γὰρ προσθήκην προσώπου ἢ ὑποστάσεως ἐπεδέξατο
ἡ ἁγία τριὰς καὶ σαρκωθέντος τοῦ ἑνὸς τῆς ἁγίας τριάδος, θεοῦ λόγου.

[2] *Liber Heracl.* B. 33 = N. 19; B. 34 = N. 20; B. 38 = N. 23.

[3] B. 360 = N. 231 (comp. note 4): *Le prosôpon de l'humanité n'est
pas odieux à la trinité*; what is said B. 33 f. = N. 20 suffices just
as little.

[4] Klostermann, 121, p. 211.

God with his *Logos* would not cease to dwell in him; for God will be all in all[1].

But I shall not discuss this longer nor enter into the question as to whether the old tradition followed by Nestorius can be accepted by us, and if so, how[2]. The main thing for me is to contrast this tradition with the trinitarian doctrine of the council of 553. Here the Holy Trinity has become something through the incarnation which it was not before[3]. As regards the time before, it is to some extent a conceivable idea, that the three ὑποστάσεις, although they are regarded as in such a way independent of each other that one alone can become man, nevertheless together make the one God; for all three ὑποστάσεις are of the same spiritual substance. But after the incarnation, the Trinity is the triad of the merely spiritual Father, of the crucified (*i.e.* the *Logos* united with human flesh, soul and intellect), and of the Spirit[4]. This understanding of the Trinity is represented by the terrible

[1] Comp. the closing sentences of Irenaeus *adv. haer.* (5. 36, 2): *Etenim unus filius, qui voluntatem patris perfecit, et unum genus humanum, in quo perficiuntur mysteria dei, quem* (read *quae*) *concupiscunt angeli videre et non praevalent investigare sapientiam dei, per quam plasma ejus conformatum et* c o n c o r p o r a t u m *filio perficitur; ut progenies ejus primogenitus* (= πρωτότοκος; hence not "*primogenita*"), *Verbum, descendat in facturam, hoc est in plasma, et capiatur ab eo, et factura iterum capiat Verbum et ascendat ad eum, supergrediens angelos, et fiet secundum imaginem et similitudinem dei.*

[2] Comp. the closing remarks in my Oberlin-lectures " *What is the truth about Jesus Christ ?* " (New York, 1913) pp. 237–241.

[3] Cp. *ibid.* p. 174.   [4] Cp. *ibid.* p. 175 note.

mediaeval pictures of the Trinity which show an old
man holding up the Crucifix by the arms of the cross
with a dove hovering above. That is certainly not
the one God of the Christian belief! Nestorius, like
Augustine, was convinced that the *opera trinitatis sunt
indivisa*[1]. And only if we go back to the old economic-
trinitarian tradition, will the trinitarian doctrine be
compatible with monotheism.

The same is to be said about the doctrine of the
incarnation. Cyril thought he had treated the idea of incarnation in a serious manner. He, too, however, did not
assume that the *Logos* was confined by the body of Jesus
during his earthly life; the *Logos* remained, according to
him, pervading the world, and this by his Godhead alone[2].
As regards the time after the ascension, the same must
be assumed. Then also in Cyril something hetero-
geneous is added to the Trinity by the manhood of
Christ and, what is still more noticeable, the idea of
incarnation appears as not sharply distinguished
from that of *inspiration*. Mythological and popular
thought may imagine an incarnation perfectly distinguished from inspiration, but the theology of the
ancient church did not dare to do so. Luther was
the first, who endeavoured to think out such a doctrine

---

[1] *Nestoriana*, p. 225, 13 ff.; *Liber Heracl.* B. 326=N. 208.
[2] ep. 17 (synodica) Migne, *ser. graeca*, 77, p. 112 c: ἐνωθεὶς γὰρ
ὁ τοῦ θεοῦ λόγος σαρκὶ καθ' ὑπόστασιν, θεὸς μέν ἐστι τῶν ὅλων, δεσπόζει δὲ
τοῦ παντός.

of incarnation, and he did this by means of his idea of
Christ's bodily ubiquity, which began with the first
moment of his conception and remained even during the
time when Christ's corpse lay in the grave.   However,
by following this line of thought, we arrive at mere
absurdities[1].   And if thus the endeavour to think out
the idea, that the *Logos* assumed the manhood in his
ὑπόστασις, leads us to absurdities, then we must go
further back than the first beginnings of this doctrine,
which are made by nothing other than the introduction
of popular mythological views into the Christian
theology.   Only by returning to the lines of the
Antiochian theology, along which in Germany *e.g.*
I. A. Dorner and M. Kaehler went and R. Seeberg
and others now are going[2], can we arrive at an understanding of the Johannine "ὁ λόγος σὰρξ ἐγένετο,"
which is in harmony with the N.T. and avoids theological
and rational impossibilities.

[1] Comp. Hauck's *Real-Encyklopädie* x, 258, 41–260, 21.
[2] Comp. the lectures mentioned above (p. 128, note 2) pp. 228–35.

INDEX OF NAMES

For EU product safety concerns, contact us at Calle de José Abascal, 56–1°,
28003 Madrid, Spain or eugpsr@cambridge.org.

www.ingramcontent.com/pod-product-compliance
Ingram Content Group UK Ltd.
Pitfield, Milton Keynes, MK11 3LW, UK
UKHW020314140625
459647UK00018B/1861